LIFE OF
BILLY DIXON

Plainsman, Scout and Pioneer

By Olive K. Dixon

Introduction by George B. Ward

Facsimile Reproduction of the Original

State✦House
Press
Mcmurry University
Abilene, Texas

Library of Congress Cataloging-in-Publication Data

Dixon, Olive K. (Olive King)
Life of "Billy" Dixon

Reprint. Previously published: Rev. ed. Dallas: P.L. Turner, 1927.
Includes index.
1. Dixon, Billy, 1850-1913. 2. Pioneers—Texas—Biography. 3. Scouts and scouting—Texas—Biography. 4. Indians of North America—Wars—1866-1898. 5. Indians of North America—Texas—Wars. 6. Frontier and pioneer life—Texas. 7. Adobe Walls, Battle of, Tex., 1874. 8. Texas History—1846-1950. I. Title.

F591.D59D58   1987   976.4'06'0924 [B]   87-42528

ISBN-13: 978-0-938349-12-9
ISBN-10: 0-938349-12-0

Printed in the United States of America

State House Press
McMurry Station, Box 637
Abilene, Texas 79697-0637
(325) 572-3974
www.mcwhiney.org/press

Distributed by Texas A&M University Press Consortium
www.tamu.edu/upress • 1-800-826-8911

Cover design by Rosenbohm Graphic Design

INTRODUCTION

One of the most romanticized chapters in the history of the United States is the story of the American West's Great Plains frontier in the decades immediately following the Civil War. It was in fact, and still is in the American imagination, the era of the dashing cowboy and the blood-stained buffalo hunter, the painted Indian warrior on horseback and the blue-suited U.S. cavalryman charging to the bugle. It was the era when Colt's revolvers blazed and Comanche lances reflected the sun against the backdrop of the Great Plains. This is the time and place that is captured vividly in the *Life of "Billy" Dixon: Plainsman, Scout and Pioneer*, a compelling narrative of the "wild, free life" on the Great Plains frontier. We ride with Billy Dixon to a high point on the plains and look out over a nearly solid mass of buffalo that stretches in every direction as far as the eye can see. We stand with Billy Dixon at Adobe Walls, in the unsettled Texas Panhandle, as hundreds of Comanche, Kiowa and Cheyenne warriors on horseback charge out of the pre-dawn darkness toward a few dozen buffalo hunters. We crouch down in desperation with Billy Dixon at the Buffalo Wallow Fight as he and a few wounded and dying men lie in a shallow depression on the plains surrounded by howling Indians on horseback. In the *Life of "Billy" Dixon* we see the Great Plains frontier through the knowing eyes of a participant who lived that frontier life and who fortunately left an accurate and engaging record for those who followed.

In the words of dime novelists, the brushstrokes of painters, and the images of movie makers, the story of the Great Plains frontier has assumed mythic proportions. Historians and participants also have often related this story in emotionally charged, romantic tones. This is appropriate, in many ways, for the story of the cowboy and the buffalo hunter, the Indian warrior and his U.S. cavalry foe, was indeed a story of immense proportions, a story of tremendous achievements and poignant tragedies, a story of inspiring courage and frightful violence, all acted out on a geographic stage of stunning size and awesome—sometimes terrible—beauty. It is not surprising therefore—in fact, it is entirely appropriate —that the story of Billy Dixon sometimes reads as if it were stolen from a formula western. A reader looking for the Wild West of fiction and film will indeed find it here, but he will find much more. He will see the grand, exciting events but he will also learn the gritty details that only a participant in such events would know—the details that make history come alive. He will see the many contradictions and complexities of life on the southwestern frontier. Billy Dixon's life story is not merely a gaudy tale of the Wild West. It is a lively, colorful portrait of men and events, with many subtle hues and shadings.

The *Life of "Billy" Dixon* acquaints the reader with a remarkable man who in a life that spanned some 63 years was a farmer, woodchopper, teamster, fur trapper, buffalo hide hunter, scout and guide for the U.S. Army, storeowner and businessman, cowboy, justice of the peace, and postmaster. His life was one of Indian fights and buffalo stampedes, brushes with death from fire and ice on the Great Plains, and encounters with men such as Bat Masterson and Quanah Parker. But it was also a life of small quiet moments, hunting alone on the plains and sleeping in a buffalo robe miles from any other man, stunned by the haunting beauty and silence of the Great Plains. Perhaps most important, Billy Dixon represents a classic American pioneer. When approaching the unknown and uncharted wilderness, he had more than a single goal in mind. As his varied careers suggest, he was seeking adventure, wealth, and opportunity, but he was also appraising the land as a businessman, entrepreneur, and settler with an eye for the land's potential development into ranches, farms, towns, and cities. In Billy Dixon we find a quintessential American frontiersman— a man with many missions, a man with many visions.

Billy Dixon was part of the generation of men and women who closed the American frontier, who brought civilization to the Texas Panhandle—one of the North America's last Indian frontiers. Yet he lived to regret the passing of the wilderness that he helped tame. In some ways, Billy Dixon was just one among many young men of his day who had the opportunity to live a life of activity and adventure. Unlike some of his fellow adventurers, however, Billy Dixon happened to be present at several pivotal moments in western history, such as the fight at Adobe Walls where the resistance and spirit of the Indians of the southern plains were symbolically broken. Billy Dixon also differed from many of his fellow buffalo hunters in that he was, by all accounts, a truly remarkable shot, a man of uncommon nerve and courage, a talented scout and guide, and a man who was able to tell his life story with accuracy and insight. Like William Frederick "Buffalo Bill" Cody—a fellow buffalo hunter, scout, and guide whom he resembled in some ways— Billy Dixon was an accomplished and capable frontiersman. A quiet and modest man, he simply never courted or encountered fame. But like Buffalo Bill, he did stand back in old age and lament the loss of the wonderful freedom of the wilderness that he had known as a young man. Billy Dixon had decidedly mixed feelings about the civilization that he had helped bring to the Great Plains.

William Dixon was born on September 25, 1850, in Ohio County, West Virginia. Orphaned at age twelve, Dixon went to live with an uncle in Ray County, Missouri, where his sister died, leaving him, as he put it, virtually "alone in the world." Like many young men in that middle western country, he could not resist the lure of the Great Plains just beyond the horizon. His imagination and dreams were fired by images of the West in the same way that earlier images of the West had inspired men to find and explore the New World, and in the same way that western images would continue to appeal to men long after the wilderness had been subdued and fenced.

In 1865, just as the end of the Civil War allowed the country to once again take up the western adventure that the war had somewhat delayed, Billy Dixon joined the wave of adventurers, dreamers, and profiteers that swept onto the plains. He was involved in many important movements and events that led to the settlement of the Great Plains within the next two decades. As an enterprising buffalo hunter, he was a significant figure in the destruction of the buffalo herds on the southern plains in the early to mid 1870s. This destruction weakened the strength and resistance of the Plains Indians whose life cycle and life style was so intimately tied to the buffalo. Billy Dixon helped usher the rancher and cowboy, farmer and shopkeeper, onto the stage once dominated by the buffalo and the Indian. Directly and indirectly he hastened the disappearance of the Indian, first as a civilian buffalo hunter (1870-1874), and later when he fought them as a scout and guide for the U.S. Cavalry (1874-1883). Symbolic of his role in successfully opposing the Indians, he was awarded the Medal of Honor by the U.S. Congress for his skill and bravery at the Buffalo Wallow Fight. But perhaps the most important thing that Billy Dixon did in his 63 years was something that he did only a few months before he died. In January 1913 he began telling the story of his life on the Great Plains to his encouraging wife, Olive King Dixon. The buffalo and Indian would have met their fates without Billy Dixon. The Texas Panhandle eventually would have been opened to the rancher and farmer without his efforts. But if he had resisted the encouragement of Olive Dixon to tell the story of his life, we would not have had his valuable information and insights into that moment in American history when the frontier finally closed.

For every important event in his life that Billy Dixon discusses at some length—the Medicine Lodge Treaty, the fights at Adobe Walls and the Buffalo Wallow—he relates numerous small moments or details of plains life that enrich our knowledge and understanding of this romanticized era. While serving as a teamster with a wagon train, he witnessed a scene worthy of Mark Twain's imagination: a caravan of ox-wagons trudging across the high plains filled only with Danish women in wooden shoes who spoke no English and were heading to Salt Lake City to become Mormons. Other unique insights are provided when Dixon delivers an ode "in honor of the buffalo chip," recounting the many uses and virtues of dried buffalo dung, and when he explains that the safest way for a man to cross a flooded river, especially a sandy one like the Cimarron, was to swim across it naked or "seize his horse's tail and follow behind."

Other small details mentioned by Billy Dixon are more serious, even haunting, such as his description of the crow—"an omen of death," he calls it—that during the thick of the deadly fight at Adobe Walls flew from building to building, in and out of the open windows, cawing raucously and never getting hit. In the aftermath of the battle, the relieved survivors were laughing and telling jokes, and "some mischevious fellow" stuck Indian skulls on each post of the corral gate. Touches such as these bring history alive, give it human resonance, although they might not even be believed if used by a western novelist or movie-maker.

Brief details or off-hand comments in the *Life of "Billy" Dixon* sometimes remind the reader of significant but often overlooked aspects of western history. Dixon mentions in passing, for instance, that for most of his career he was employed by the United States government as a teamster, guide, scout, or postmaster. We often fail to recognize that from the time of Lewis and Clark to that of Buffalo Bill, many of the great figures on the American frontier were agents of the federal government.

Despite the popular image of free-lance pioneers and rugged individualists opening and settling the West, many pioneers were on the frontier as part of a grand, national scheme of exploration and development—funded by military and scientific branches of the government— aimed at exploring, mapping, evaluating, developing, and ultimately claiming the West as part of an American empire. Billy Dixon's individual initiative, skill, and bravery notwithstanding, the bulk of his colorful western career was in the service of enormous bureaucratic organizations. The individual heroics of pioneering men and women made a significant difference on the cutting edge of the frontier, but they must be seen against a background of organized, institutional activity.

In his life story, Billy Dixon's vision is filtered through several lenses—that of his wife, who patiently wrote down his lengthy oral history, and that of Frederick S. Barde who took Mrs. Dixon's voluminous notes and edited them into the first edition published in 1914 under the title *Life and Adventures of "Billy" Dixon of Adobe Walls, Texas Panhandle.* The revised edition of 1927, which is reprinted here, added a brief introduction by historian Joseph B. Thoburn, changed the title and some of the illustrations, and rearranged a few paragraphs. It is, however, essentially the same book as the 1914 edition. Billy Dixon died in 1913, before the project was finished, so his "autobiography", which reads as though told in his own words, appeared with the polished glow of a ghostwriter who was sometimes afflicted with the disease of purple prose. The book accurately reflects Dixon's memories and opinions but is unlikely that the taciturn Billy Dixon would have described ducks and

geese landing at Buffalo Springs by saying: "In Fall and
Spring, migratory water-fowl descend to desport themselves in the pools." In later years, when readers asked
Olive Dixon if her husband had used such flowery
language she acknowledged that the words were doctored,
but she was adamant that the details of the events and
the thoughts and interpretations were only those of her
husband: "The book was made by Billy Dixon."

From the earliest pages of the book, Billy Dixon makes
it clear that he was well aware of the often distorted
images of the frontier West and the men and women
who settled it. That was one reason why he wanted to set
the record straight in his own book. But Billy Dixon
cheerfully admits that he participated in some of the
distorted images himself. He describes with amusement
how as fourteen-year-old bull-whackers (freight wagon
drivers) he and a friend invested their riches in those
things that they knew would make them true westerners:
an oversized cowboy hat, Colt's revolver, butcher knife,
and bull whip. "I doubt if two boys ever felt more
important. I am sure that the older men must have smiled
at the two youngsters, each buried beneath his big hat
and leaning to one side under the weight of his 'shooting
irons.'" The widespread use and power of western
images in post-Civil War America is repeatedly illustrated
in Dixon's narrative. A tenderfoot from the East named
Fairchild showed up one day in clothes that marked him
as the quintessential eastern dandy, including "a flower-
bed vest and a cravat that resembled a Rocky Mountain
sunset." Fairchild's uncontrollable eagerness to shoot
buffalo and fight Indians with buffalo hunters led him to
convert himself overnight from exotic eastern dandy to

absurd western dude in boots, spurs, a sombrero "wide enough for an umbrella", a brilliant bandana, and a cartridge belt stuffed with ammunition for his new six-shooter and 50 calibre buffalo rifle.

Many times during his career, Billy Dixon himself encountered or utilized western stereotypes. In his first months on the Plains, Billy was disappointed at how unwild the West sometimes was. He delighted in the feeling of danger from Indians on an early freighting trip from Omaha to Colorado, but was severely disappointed when his stereotyped expectations went unfulfilled. They saw no Indians or buffalo on the entire trip, although the old timers took advantage of the pilgrims' naivete by crying out warnings of impending Indian attacks. Billy and his compatriots eventually played similar tricks on other gullible tenderfeet. The dandy-turned-cowboy Fairchild was so anxious to have a violent encounter with Indians that he became a nuisance and a potential danger. To cure him of this reckless desire, which no doubt came from reading too many dime novels, Bat Masterson and a few other practical jokers staged a frightening mock Indian attack that caused the panicked Fairchild to ride frantically for camp with bullets flying about his head. The elaborate stunt worked —and ended the chagrined Fairchild's childish fantasies about what was in fact a serious reality of plains life. On another occasion Billy and fellow scout Jack Stilwell staged a prank that shocked an army officer they were guiding from Camp Supply, Indian Territory, to Dodge City, Kansas. An excellent shot, Billy played on the officer's exaggerated image of hard-bitten frontiersmen by shooting at Stilwell's ears with his rifle. His close shots and Stilwell's effective acting convinced the appalled officer that wild man Billy was actually knicking Stilwell's ear with each shot.

Behind the jokes and facades, Billy Dixon was a tough and resourceful frontier character. With his remarkable shooting and scouting ability, his muscular frame, long dark hair, and tight-lipped personality, he lived up to the stereotypical frontier image portrayed in folklore and in the popular media. Yet the complex man who is revealed in the *Life of "Billy" Dixon* defies many commonly held stereotypes. This tough frontiersman and Indian fighter who brought the seeds of civilization to the Great Plains—particularly to the Texas Panhandle—was quite sympathetic to the Indians he was displacing, and he seriously regretted the passing of the wilderness and the free hunting life:

> ... no man is ever quite his former self after he has felt deeply the bigness, the silence and the mystery of that region ... The heart swells with emotion at re-membrance of the wild, free life along those old trails, and knowledge that they have vanished forever brings a feeling of deep regret.

Even though some of Dixon's elegaic comments about the Indians and the old days on the plains can be written off to romanticism and middle-aged nostalgia, his feelings are stated often and have an emphatic sincerity. His longing backward glances are typical of those found in the reminiscences of many other men who lived the frontier life—men as diverse as Buffalo Bill Cody and Theodore Roosevelt. His attitudes are also reflected widely in American culture—in art, literature, and folk-lore. At least since James Fenimore Cooper, Americans have responded positively to two conflicting values: The sense that the wilderness is the precious source of the unique American experience and character, and the contradictory notion that it is our God-given destiny to conquer that wilderness and replace it with the blessings of a new American civilization. Billy Dixon—quintessential frontiersman and quintessential American—lived and embodied those contradictory values.

The *Life of "Billy" Dixon* abounds in contradictions. That is not to say that Billy Dixon could not get his story straight. It is to say that the American West—like life itself—was an experience of extremes and complexities. It is the expression of these complexities and contradictions by an important participant in the settling of the West that makes this book so valuable. Billy Dixon saw Indians as "rascals" capable of "evil and horrible" crimes. He fought and killed Indians on several occasions. Yet he also regarded Indians as people of dignity and pride who were cruelly victimized by the white man's diseases and the white man's refusal to live up to treaty obligations. He did not hesitate to mention "naked and mangled bodies of white men who had been spread-eagled and tortured with steel and fire", but neither did he hesitate to describe how Indian women and children were killed "with utmost cruelty" at Sand Creek, Colorado, by white men. Billy Dixon's eloquent descriptions of the "free, open life" of the plains frontier presents a picture of a life of freedom and exhilaration:

> In after years I thought many times of that night on
> the Plains . . . Save for the occasional howling of
> wolves and coyotes, the night was supernaturally
> silent. It was the stillness of the primeval solitude. It

> was the stuff that makes a man in a warm bed under
> a roof feel like getting up to saddle his horse and ride
> away to this Land of Nowhere. Once in the blood, it
> can never be lost.

This from a man who frequently described agonizing experiences with "killing cold" on the plains: "I once made a ride with dispatches, and became so stiff with cold . . . that I could not dismount from my horse—I simply let go and fell off."

Similar contradictions are found in other descriptions of plains life, especially its natural beauty. Dixon describes himself as "a youthful Daniel Boone . . . I was happiest when ranging the open country with my gun on my shoulder and a dog at my heels, far out among the wild birds and the wild animals." Describing his life as a buffalo hunter in the 1870s, he similarly commented, "Round us rolled the interminable Plains, arched by the glittering sky, and in the fire-light the rollicking buffalo hunters sang and danced . . . Just to feel one's self living in that country was a joy." Such sentiments often run head on into Dixon's frank descriptions of the danger and violence that coexisted with the beauty and freedom of plains' life. While guiding the U.S. Cavalry across Texas's Staked Plains during the summer of 1877, the troops and some buffalo hunters nearly died of thirst.

> The sufferings of both men and horses were terrible,
> and all the way to the Double Lakes our trail was
> strewn with cast-off clothing and equipment. The
> buffalo hunters were in no less desperate straits,
> many of them, like the soldiers, dropping down to
> die along the way. Horses were killed that their
> blood might be drunk to assuage the fever of burning
> throats and tongues.

Sometimes Dixon captured the contradictions of the plains experience in a single situation: grass fires on the plains, for instance, were at once "a magnificent spectacle" and "terrifying." "Carried forward in the teeth of a high, boisterous wind, the fire was appalling, and there was something sinister and somber in the low roar that sent terror to the heart of wild animals."Yet a sentence later he noted,"At night when the wind was still, a fire on the Plains was a beautiful sight. In the far distance, the tongues of flame appeared so small that they looked like a red line of countless fingers, pointing with trembling motion toward the sky." Dixon's ability to express both the beauty and horror of life on the plains makes this book a refreshing source of information.

Dixon is always frank with the reader. He admits that when he was a young bull-whacker driving freight wagons, some of the men would steal an occasional chicken or pig "in a spirit of mischief." And he added that "it would be useless for me to say that I did not help eat from many a well-filled pot." Sometimes his frankness addressed more serious questions: "No mercy was shown the buffalo . . . . I killed as many as my three men could handle, working them as hard as they were willing to work. This was deadly business, without sentiment; it was dollars against tenderheartedness, and dollars won." Despite this frank talk, and the cool tone, the rugged frontiersman had a tenderhearted side when it came to buffalo. He objected to the wanton destruction of these valuable animals and he regretted their passing, but like virtually all those who lived on the frontier, in the end he opted for civilization.

An important figure easily overlooked in the pages of the *Life of "Billy" Dixon* is the person ultimately responsible for the book: Olive King Dixon. This Panhandle pioneer was born on Bent Mountain in Virginia, January 30, 1873, just about the time that her future husband and his fellow hide hunters were moving into the Panhandle for the last phase of buffalo hunting on the southern plains. Olive King's brother Archie had left Virginia for the Texas Panhandle like many other Southerners who saw promise in the Old South's new frontier: the Lone Star State. In 1892 Archie invited his sister to visit his sod house in Hutchinson County near the Adobe Walls country. The idea appealed to her and in April, 1893, Olive King left the green softness of Virginia for the rugged brown plains of Texas. Once on the high plains, Olive King knew that she had found her home, her heart's country. Despite the disappearance of the buffalo and the Indians, and despite the presence of railroads, wind mills, and barbed wire, the Panhandle was still an isolated frontier compared to most of the rest of the country. Olive King was not intimidated by the country or its spirited people for long.

After working as a teacher in the Panhandle for a few months, Olive King met modest, soft-spoken Billy Dixon, the leathery frontiersman whom she had heard so much about. In the summer of 1894, they were married, and over the next several years raised a family of four children. From time to time during these years a bit of plains' history would appear in print that dealt with Billy Dixon or an event that he participated in. Sometimes the history would be in error or wildly exaggerated. When Frederick S. Barde, an author and editor from Guthrie,

Oklahoma, wrote to the Dixons for information about Billy's life, they wrote back inquiring if Barde might write a history based on the life of Billy Dixon. Barde was unable to get involved at that time, but he suggested that Mrs. Dixon take notes while Mr. Dixon reminisced. Starting in January, 1913, Olive Dixon began taking down, in laborious longhand, a year by year recital of her husband's eventful life. On March 9, 1913, only two months after she had started dogging him about with pad and pencil in hand, Billy Dixon died of pneumonia. In June, Barde saw the notebooks of reminiscences and felt that with a bit of polish they could be published. With Barde's help, the work was edited and published, coming off the press in 1914. The book was well received and much appreciated by scholars and general readers alike. It was revised and reprinted in 1927, and remains a classic book of the southwestern frontier. A new genera-tion of readers will meet Billy Dixon in this 1987 reprint.

From the time she began writing down her husband's reminiscences in 1913 until her death in 1954, Olive King Dixon attempted to preserve the history of her husband and the land they knew and loved so well. While struggling to keep her young family together, Mrs. Dixon began researching and writing western history, often as a reporter for Panhandle newspapers. When the Panhandle-Plains Historical Society came into being in 1922, Olive Dixon was there. She both lived the frontier life, and helped preserve it for future generations. She saw to it that historical monuments were placed at Adobe Walls and at the site of the Buffalo Wallow Fight. And in 1929, Olive Dixon had her beloved husband reburied with full military honors at a spot that had been central to his life and to the life of the Texas Panhandle: Adobe Walls. This remarkable woman, herself a Panhandle pioneer, saw to it that her husband's life and knowledge were preserved—in memory and in the words of the *Life of "Billy" Dixon.*

Olive Dixon's book tells many tales about her husband, but the pivotal story of the narrative is Billy Dixon's lengthy description of the fight at Adobe Walls in the rugged and isolated Texas Panhandle. The inability of hundreds of plains warriors to defeat a few dozen buffalo hunters symbolized the beginning of the end for the Indian tribes who had ruled the high plains of Texas. The original Adobe Walls was a trading post built about 1843 on the South Canadian River in the northern Texas Panhandle by William Bent, the fur trader of the Great Plains and Rocky Mountains. In 1874 a number of buffalo hunters and businessmen established a small trading town about a mile away to serve the needs of the buffalo hunters who were following the disappearing herds into the Panhandle where they still roamed. This new collection of sod and picket buildings and corrals was named Adobe Walls after the ruins of the original fort and trading post. In 1874 this part of the plains was still largely controlled by Indians. It was extremely dangerous country for buffalo hunters but, because the herds else-where on the southern plains had been decimated, the northern Panhandle was one of the last places in North America where buffalo could be found in great numbers.

For centuries buffalo had been killed by Indians and white hunters for more than sustenance. From the seventeenth century on, buffalo robes and meat—and eventually hides—had been an important element in the trade relationships between Indians, French voyageurs, American mountain men, and the huge trapping and trading concerns of North America, including the Hudson's Bay Company, The American Fur Company, and others. The buffalo robe, like the better known beaver pelt, was an important element in the economics of western North America. In the early nineteenth century, the hunting of buffalo switched from what William Hornaday called "desultory destruction" to "systematic slaughter." The coming of the railroads to the Great Plains in the mid-to-late 1860s accelerated the slaughter. Free-lance buffalo hunters quickly gave way to merchants and entrepreneurs who supplied arms, ammunition, and provisions to organized groups of hunters. The single biggest factor in the destruction of the buffalo was the discovery in 1871 that buffalo hides were an acceptable source of leather. Up to this point, buffalo had been taken largely for meat and robes. As soon as it became known that a leather gold mine was available in the hides, the true slaughter began.

Billy Dixon had been a fur trapper and market hunter for some time, selling beaver pelts or elk for what they would bring, but with buffalo hides now so valuable, he switched to full-time buffalo hunting. The era of the buffalo hide hunters was beginning. They descended on the plains in great numbers, decimating the herds. The slaughter was almost unimaginable. For several years in the early 1870s buffalo were killed at an astonishing rate that averages out to over 200 per hour, twenty-four hours a day, day-in and day-out. It is no wonder that by 1874 the southern plains were barren of buffalo in many areas where they had recently blackened the earth. The

Texas Panhandle, the site of the new Adobe Walls, was where the buffalo made their last stand on the southern Great Plains and it was where Billy Dixon and other daring hide hunters headed.

The Indians were not pleased with this new development, and some buffalo hunters paid for their daring with their lives. The spring of 1874 brought more and more hide hunters into the Panhandle, and the Indians increased their "depredations" on the hunters' isolated camps. The uneasy buffalo hunters did not want to abandon this last lucrative buffalo range and stubbornly remained in the area, but many, including Billy Dixon, came into Adobe Walls from the surrounding country for protection when Indian resistance was strong. Billy Dixon spent June 26, 1874, buying supplies in Adobe Walls in preparation for two months of buffalo hunting in an area northwest of Adobe Walls that Dixon believed was free of Indians. The Indian troubles of some weeks earlier were forgotten, and the twenty-eight men and one woman at Adobe Walls the evening of June 26 were not expecting trouble. About two o'clock in the morning, a loud crack like the sound of a rifle awakened a few men sleeping in Hanrahan's sod house saloon. The big cottonwood ridge pole which supported the dirt roof had mysteriously cracked. Soon about fifteen men were up trying to repair the ridge pole. By the time the job was done, the sky was growing red in the east, and Billy Dixon decided not to go back to sleep. Just as he was gathering his gear, he noticed something moving vaguely in the dusky distance, but could not at first see what the objects were. "Then I was thunderstruck," he reported later.

The black body of moving objects suddenly spread
out like a fan, and from it went up one single, solid
yell—a war-whoop that seemed to shake the very air
of the early morning. Then came the thundering roar
of running horses, and the hideous cries of each of
the individual warriors who engaged in the onslaught. I could see that hundreds of Indians were
coming.

The Battle of Adobe Walls had begun. Billy Dixon
describes in graphic detail how the handful of buffalo
hunters, greatly outnumbered and isolated on the plains
in a few sod structures, held off hundreds of Kiowa,
Cheyenne, and Comanche warriors with their buffalo
guns. On the third day, after the fighting had essentially
ended, a group of about fifteen Indians appeared on a
distant bluff nearly a mile away. Several of the hunters
suggested that Dixon, a crack shot, shoot at these Indians
with his big "50" Sharps rifle. From this virtually impossible distance, Dixon knocked an Indian from his horse
with the buffalo rifle that awed Indians sometimes said
"Shoots today-Kills tomorrow." Although Dixon dis-
counted it as a lucky shot, this remarkable moment of
western drama symbolized the skill of men like Dixon
and the desperate straits of their Indian counterparts.

Within weeks of the battle at Adobe Walls, Billy Dixon
was employed as a U.S. army scout by General Nelson
A. Miles who was a primary field commander in the Red
River War (1874-1875) which broke the strength of the
Kiowa and Comanche in the Texas Panhandle. Dixon
helped select the site of Fort Elliott in that rugged Indian
country, and was attached to the post for duty. In 1883,
less than a decade later, Billy Dixon returned to civilian
life and homesteaded land that took in the site of the

original Adobe Walls. There he built his ranch house; and there in 1893, near the site of the grim battle, he met and married his wife and raised his children. He was made postmaster of Adobe Walls and served in that position for twenty years. Like the disappearance of the buffalo and the Indians from the Texas Panhandle, the fact that Billy Dixon later worked there as a cowboy, farmer, and postmaster, and then married Olive King and raised a family there, symbolizes the abrupt and dramatic changes on the Great Plains frontier.

For the general public in the late nineteenth century, some of this symbolism was decidedly negative. Unfortunately for the buffalo hide hunter, he had the misfortune to virtually eliminate an animal which had come to represent and embody the American West. The hide hunter appeared at a time in the 1870s and 1880s when the American Indian, wilderness, and wildlife were fading from the scene, and when the rapidly growing urban population was beginning to develop strong romantic yearnings for nature, wilderness, the Indian— and the buffalo—now that they were comfortably distant and clearly subdued. An entire bundle of issues that arose in the post-Civil War years—conservation, the plight of the Indian, the fading frontier—came to be dramatically symbolized in the disappearing buffalo. And the only obvious villian was the hide hunter.

Pointing the finger of blame and shame at the buffalo hunter was not entirely fair. The hide hunter was only one of many post-Civil War entrepreneurs exploiting the natural resources of the West. Like the miner or the logger the buffalo hunter produced great wealth and great waste. He was essentially a laborer in a competitive economic structure, one link in a national chain of agricultural and industrial development that included railroads, ranching, mining, and the expanding economies of coal, steel, and petroleum. The buffalo hunter was in many ways not so different from the beaver-trapping Rocky Mountain hunters of the early-to-mid nineteenth century, or even the Daniel Boone-style hunters of the Appalachian frontier in the late 1700s. All of these hunters were, in part, in it for the profit. They were all an opening wedge for civilization, and they all served as agents of corporations seeking to make gains from furs, forests, and land. The buffalo hunters—the Billy Dixons— were the last in the line of American frontier hunter figures, and they happened to hunt an animal with great popular and symbolic appeal. As a result, the buffalo hunters paid a price—they came to be portrayed as ghouls in greasy, blood-stained pants, killing the noble buffalo for profit.

Billy Dixon helps correct and balance the picture. We come to know him as a man of courage, skill, and intelligence: a man of honor and insight. We can picture him sitting in his ranch house or post office at Adobe Walls—"The land of my boyhood dreams," he called it—and know that he too was deeply saddened by the passing of the western frontier. Billy Dixon realized that he was in part responsible for destroying what he so deeply loved:

> I fear that the conquest of savagery in the Southwest was due more often to love of adventure than to any wish that cities should arise in the desert, or that the highways of civilization should take the place of the trails of the Indian and the buffalo. In fact, many of us

believed and hoped that the wilderness would remain forever. Life there was to our liking.

Despite the advantages of "higher civilization," Billy Dixon's knowledge that the "wild, free life" had "vanished forever brings a feeling of deep regret . . . that something worthwhile has been lost." When asked in later years about his experiences on the frontier, he often detected an implication that the hardships of plains life must have been unbearable. His response was straightforward and simple:

> Gladly would I live it all over again, such is my cast of mind and my hunger for the freedom of the big wide place. I would run the risks and endure all the hardships that were naturally ours just for the contentment and freedom to be found in such an outdoor life. I should be unspeakably happy once more to feast on buffalo meat and other wild game cooked on a camp-fire, to eat sour dough biscuit and drink black coffee from a quart tin cup.

We can see Billy Dixon, standing out by a corral near the sites of his buffalo hunting and Indian fighting, as his wife Olive takes down his wistful thoughts about a frontier life now gone. We can imagine Billy Dixon, standing in the land of his boyhood dreams, a middle-aged man only weeks from death, his mind ranging over the details of his life, his memories running back to the free, wild life that he helped bring to an end.

George B. Ward
Texas State Historical Association
January, 1987

LIFE OF
"BILLY" DIXON

BILLY DIXON, SCOUT, IN HIS PRIME

LIFE OF
"BILLY" DIXON

PLAINSMAN, SCOUT AND PIONEER

*A Narrative in which are Described Many Things Relating
to the Early Southwest, with an Account of the
Fights Between Indians and Buffalo Hunters
at Adobe Walls and at Buffalo Wallow,
for which Congress voted the Medal
of Honor to the Survivors*

BY

OLIVE K. DIXON

REVISED EDITION

P. L. TURNER COMPANY
Publishers

DALLAS   TEXAS

PREFACE

"I FEAR," said "Billy" Dixon, half humorously, "that the conquest of savagery in the Southwest was due more often to love of adventure than to any wish that cities should arise in the desert, or that the highways of civilization should take the place of the trails of the Indian and the buffalo. In fact, many of us believed and hoped that the wilderness would remain forever. Life there was to our liking. Its freedom, its dangers, its tax upon strength and courage, gave a zest to living, especially to young men, unapproached by anything to be found in civilized communities. Therefore, let it be said that if there was bravery and heroism, it came less by design than it did from the emergencies of accident and surroundings, and that usually it was spontaneous."

The pioneers themselves were not inclined to feel that their exploits were so extraordinary as to be of use in the making of books. Their long abode in silent places made them taciturn; and their lack of liberal knowledge of the rules of writing and their unwillingness to risk the appearance of conceit left them reluctant to relate their adventures for the printed page.

Posterity, however, has a claim upon these forerunners that may not be lightly thrust aside. The history of this struggle to subdue the wild places should be preserved and can be gathered only from the lips or the records of participants. In a few years the latter will have all vanished, as the frontier itself has faded into a memory. From camp-fire tales have grown the legends of heroes.

After withstanding for many years the solicitation of friends and early associates, Billy Dixon consented to the publication of such of his experiences on the frontier as he believed might be of interest to those persons who find pleasure in reading of the perils and hardships encountered by men and women who forsook the comforts of more civilized surroundings to risk their lives in making habitable the wilderness—and in securing space and adventure.

Though a taciturn man, Mr. Dixon made strong friendships and entertained the warmest affection for the men with whom he had been associated in pioneer days. Mr. W. B. ("Bat") Masterson, writing from New York City, a short time before his death, said:

"I first became acquainted with Billy Dixon on the buffalo range in the fall of 1872 and continued to know him well and intimately for several years thereafter. The last time I saw him was at Sweetwater, a small hamlet just off the Military Reservation at Fort Elliott, Texas, then called Cantonment, in the spring of 1876.

"Billy Dixon was a typical frontiersman of the

highest order. The perils and hardships of border
life were exactly suited to his stoical and imperturb-
able nature. This does not mean that Billy was not
a kind-hearted, generous and hospitable man, for
he possessed all these admirable qualities to a high
degree, but he was cool, calculating and uncom-
municative at all times.

"I was with Billy in the fight at Adobe Walls
in June, 1874, between the buffalo-hunters and that
fierce band of warriors composed of the best fighting men of the Cheyenne, Arapahoe, Comanche
and Kiowa tribes, numbering fully one thousand
braves. Billy and I occupied the same window the
first day of the battle and I hope we did our share
in the fight. Billy was an extraordinarily fine shot
with a buffalo-gun and he never overlooked an opportunity that first day to demonstrate his unerr-
ing aim whenever and wherever an Indian showed
his head. We were scouts together afterwards in
General Miles' command which left Fort Dodge,
Kansas in the early part of August, the same year,
for the Panhandle country, where the hostiles were
assembled in great numbers. While I was not with
him, I am quite familiar with all the details of the
fight in the buffalo wallow on the north bank of
the Washita River in which Billy and Amos Chapman and four soldiers stood off a large band of
hostiles for an entire day. It was largely due to
Billy's heriosm on that occasion that the party was
saved from complete annihilation."

The publication of this volume was decided upon

in the fall of 1912. Mr. Dixon was in vigorous health, and became greatly interested in the undertaking. His memory was remarkable for its tenacity, which enabled him to recall the past with ease and accuracy.

At our home on our claim in Cimarron County, I took down from his dictation the greater and the essential part of the present narrative. I kept note-books in every room, and sometimes carried them to the corral, that I might be in readiness to set down what my husband might say as he was moved by reflection or inquiry to talk of the past. Many of his pioneer friends learned of his plans, and encouraged him to persevere until the work should be accomplished. The material grew until there was an armful of manuscript, and the ground had been fairly covered.

Little did we suspect that Death—the enemy from whom he had escaped so many times in the old days—was at hand, and that the arrow was set to the bow. During a winter storm early in 1913 he was suddenly stricken. He went unwillingly and complainingly to his bed, regretting that what he believed was a trivial illness should pull down a man who never before had known a day's sickness. Pneumonia developed, and he expired March 9, 1913, insisting with his last breath that he would recover. Interment took place in the cemetery at Texline, Texas, under the auspices of the local Masonic Lodge. Mr. Dixon for many years had been a consistent member of that order.

In the publication of this volume, I wish to acknowledge my obligations to Mr. Frederick S. Barde, of Guthrie, Oklahoma, who compiled the manuscript and carried the book through the first edition, and also to those pioneers of the Panhandle, Mr. Chas. Goodnight and Mr. James H. Cator, friends of many years, whose counsel and suggestions were helpful in many ways.

THE AUTHOR.

CONTENTS

xi

LIST OF ILLUSTRATIONS

INTRODUCTION

THE stories of pioneers and of pioneer life are filled with interest for the patriotic American. Unfortunately, comparatively few pioneers personally recorded an account of their experiences. Indeed, much that has been written concerning the pioneering incidents of the region east of the Alleghenies, and even east of the Mississippi, was handed down orally for several generations before it was finally reduced to writing. In this, the region west of the Mississippi seems to have fared better in that the literature of its pioneering period is relatively much more abundant than in the older states.

William Dixon was naturally not only a man of few words, but, last and least of all the themes for his conversation were his own adventures and exploits. Even his wife learned of these only by hearsay from others and she found him very reluctant to speak of them when they were brought to his attention. It was therefore but natural that he should have scouted the idea of putting his reminiscences into book form, and the fact that he finally consented to do so bears eloquent witness to the patient, persistent and persuasive influence of his wife, who, having decided that his story should be thus preserved, refused to be discouraged in the effort to collect and record the details which in the aggregate were necessary to make it complete.

The reader will readily understand that it had been planned to publish the work in the form of an autobiographic narrative. The death of Mr. Dixon before the completion of the book rendered this impossible. Mrs. Dixon, who had inspired him to make the attempt and who had been his amanuensis throughout the dictation and recording of his statements, naturally assumed the authorship. It is a plain story, simply told, with no effort at embellishment, though such a story needs no embellishment. The historical literature of the Great Plains is enriched by such a contribution.

JOSEPH B. THOBURN.

LIFE OF "BILLY" DIXON

CHAPTER I

IN no other country could there have been found a region so inviting, so alluring, so fascinating, to the spirit of adventure as the Great Plains. How it gripped the imagination of young men, sons of pioneers, between the Mississippi and the Alleghenies, in those early days! How it called to them, and beckoned to them to forsake their homes and journey westward into the unknown!

Vast and undisturbed, it stretched from the British Possession to the Rio Grande. It was a natural stage on which was enacted the most picturesque and romantic drama of the nineteenth century. Its background was the Rocky Mountains, from whose towering ramparts the Plains swept down toward the east, giving an unobstructed view of the stirring panorama that for more than half a century was unrivalled for its scenes of daring and conquest.

The Plains were marvelously adapted to the needs of uncivilized people, who derived their sustenance from the bounty of the wilderness, and to

the heavy increase and perpetuation of the animal
life upon which they subsisted. Upon its level
floors, enemies or game could be seen from afar, an
advantage in both warfare and hunting. The
natural grasses were almost miraculously disposed
to the peculiarities of soil and climate, affording
the richest pasturage in the green of summer and
becoming even more nutritious as the seasons advanced toward the snows of winter. This insured
the presence of enormous numbers of herbivorous
animals, such as the buffalo, the antelope and the
deer, from which the Indian derived his principal
food and fashioned his garments and his shelter.
His only toil was the chase with its splendid excitement, and his only danger the onslaught of
tribal enemies. The climate was healthful and invigorating. In all the world could not have been
found a more delightful home for primitive men.

That the Indian should have resisted with
relentless and increasing ferocity every effort to
drive him from this paradise was natural and jus-
tifiable from his point of view. In those days, he
felt that to go elsewhere meant starvation and
death for his family and tribe. Above all, he firmly
believed that the country was his, as it had been
from the beginning, and that the white man was
cruel, merciless and wrong in depriving him of his
old home—a home that the white man did not need
and would not use.

North and south across this gigantic stage the
teeming animal life of the Plains, especially the

buffaloes, moved regularly with the procession of the equinoxes. The first grass of spring to which the Cheyennes gave the poetic name, *mah-nah-see-tah*—had scarcely made green the landscape before it was darkened with moving herds northward bound, in obedience to the primal instinct that pulses more deeply with the coming of spring. The pastures were endless, and the moist earth vibrant with the sounds of the fresh season. Everywhere wild flowers were springing from the sod. The water-holes were full, and the sandy rivers flashed in the sunshine. Clouds of water-fowl swirled and descended upon the bars, to rest in their flight to their nesting grounds. The eagle in the sky and the lark in the grass were alike free to raise their young, far from the intrusion of man. The Indians, with their women, children, dogs and ponies, moving dimly on the far-off Plains, were native to the scene, and passed unnoticed by the other denizens of the solitude.

Once more the pageant of the wilderness moved on its mysterious way, this time from north to south. The storms of spring and summer had rolled their thunder through the solitude and reddened the sky with their lightning. The rains had spent themselves. The season of creation and growth had passed. The Plains were shaggy with brown grass. Soon frost would sharpen the air, and snow come on the cold winds and whiten the earth. The buffaloes, the deer and the antelope had thicker and warmer coats; the bear was growing drowsy, and hunting his winter cave; the wild turkey flashed a finer bronze; the prairie chicken, the crane, the mallard and the goose were fat and succulent beyond other days.

Of all this domain the Indian was lord and master. There was none to dispute his sway. The stars in the sky were his night companions, and the sun his supreme benefactor by day. All were his servants. His race multiplied and was happy. Food and shelter were to be found upon every hand. The white man had not come, bringing disease and poverty.

In savagery, a more delightful existence could not be found. What joy of physical living, with strength, health and contentment in every village. There were wars, to be sure, but feats of daring appealed to the brave, and there was love of fame and honor, just as there was inside the walled cities beyond the Atlantic, where, from a comparative standpoint, men were less civilized than their western brothers who fought with bow and arrow, war club and tomahawk.

The fruitful summers were given over to idling in pleasant places—in a village beside a stream, or in the foothills of the mountains. There were singing and dancing and the telling of old tales. The women looked after the household, ever watchful of the little girls and the young women of marriageable age. The plaintive notes of the love-flute could be heard in the dusk of twilight. The warriors trained the boys and the young men in horsemanship and the use of arms, subjecting them to tests of physical endurance, even pain, that they might grow to be strong, invincible men.

There is something beyond description that clutches a man's heart and imagination in the Plains country. Whether it is the long sweep of the horizon, with its suggestion of infinity, touching upon melancholy, or that wide-arching expanse of sky, glittering by night and glorious by day, may not be determined, yet no man is ever quite his former self after he has felt deeply the bigness, the silence and the mystery of that region.

Trackless and boundless, the Great Plains at first offered to the adventurous traveler the many dangers that come from losing one's way in the wilderness. The sun and the stars were guides for direction, but not for water, wood and pasture. Travel was not made certain and continuous until countless feet and hoofs and wheels had worn trails. The making of trails is one of the most primitive acts of man, and it seems incredible that the first were blazed within such recent times in this country. The most noted of all these trails was the Santa Fe Road or Trail that led to Santa Fe, New Mexico, from Westport, Mo., where it was joined by smaller highways from points in the surrounding country.

The heart swells with emotion at remembrance of the wild, free life along those old trails, and knowledge that they have vanished forever brings a feeling of deep regret. Railroads, to be sure, meet modern needs, and have changed the wilderness into gardens, but, nevertheless, beyond and above all these demands of a higher civilization, with its commerce and its feverish haste, remains the thought that something worth while has been lost, at least to those who found joy in braving dangers and in overcoming the obstacles of primitive conditions. What a living, moving, thrilling panorama stretched along the old trails! How vast the wealth that rolled past!

The end came when the Santa Fe railroad reached Raton in 1880. Thenceforward, wind and rain and the encroaching grass began their work of obliteration. Only gashed river banks and scarred hillsides guard from the destroying years the last vestiges of what once were a nation's highways. The snowswept summits of the Spanish Peaks look down no more upon the crawling ox-trains, nor does the swart Apache watch stealthily on Rabbit Ear Mountain to see if a weakly guarded train is coming down the Santa Fe Road. There are two pretty Spanish names for Spanish Peaks—"Las Cumbres Españolas" and "Las dos Hermanas," (The Two Sisters). The Ute name is "Wahtoya" (The Twins).

CHAPTER II

I WAS born in Ohio County, West Virginia, September 25, 1850, the oldest of three children. My mother died when her third child was born. I was then ten years old. I believe that the earliest remembrances of one's mother make the deepest impression. In the few years that I received my mother's care, my character was given a certain trend that it never lost. My mother told me that I should always be kind to dumb animals, and especially to birds. In all my after life I never forgot her words. Often on the Plains and in the wilderness did I turn my horse or wagon aside rather than injure a road lizard or a terrapin that was unable to get out of the way.

When I was twelve years old my father died, and with my sister I went to live with my uncle, Thomas Dixon, who lived in Ray County, Missouri. In those days travel was difficult, and Missouri seemed a long way from our home in West Virginia. We had been with our uncle only a few months when my sister was stricken with typhoid fever, and died after an illness of about two weeks. This left me alone in the world. My uncle was kind and good to me, but I stayed with him only a year. I was a strong, rugged boy, un-

willing to be dependent upon even a kinsman for
my living, and with much resolution I decided to
seek my own fortune.

While at my uncle's home I had often met men
who had been to the far west, and their marvelous
tales of adventure fired my imagination, and filled
me with eagerness to do what they had done. My
dreams were filled with beautiful pictures of that
dim region that lay toward the Rocky Mountains.

In those days no traveler undertook this westward journey without a horse and a gun. I was
penniless, and the purchase of these necessities
seemed utterly beyond my resources.

I had formed the acquaintance of a boy named
Dan Keller, several years older than myself, and
also without father or mother. Many times had
we talked of the wild country where game
abounded and Indian warriors rode as free as the
wind. That we should go was as inevitable as the
coming of the grass in spring or the falling of
leaves in autumn. My uncle would have been
greatly opposed to our enterprise had we told him
of it, so I went away without telling him good bye.

Having no horses, Dan and I started on foot,
and in place of guns we had only courage and our
chubby fists. In a sack on my back I carried my
one extra shirt and my mother's photograph. The
latter I treasured beyond all my other possessions.
Making our way to the Missouri River we fell in
with some wood choppers who were supplying with
fuel the steamboats that in those days plied that

river. The camps of these wood choppers were found at frequent intervals along the shore. The men were rough but generous and hospitable, and we were welcomed at their camps, many of which we reached at night-fall. We hunted and trapped up and down the river for several months, often staying in one camp for a couple of weeks.

We were beginning to see the world and to find adventure. Around the campfires at night the wood choppers told of their exploits in the west— of how they had hunted the grizzly bear, the buffalo, the panther, the deer and the antelope, of how they had been caught in the howling blizzards, of their narrow escapes from drowning in swollen rivers, and of the battles they had fought with hostile Indians. Many times we sat and listened until midnight, the rush of the river sounding in our ears, and then after we had gone to bed we lay looking at the stars and wondering if it would ever be possible for us to lead such a delightful life.

Following the wood cutters' camps up the great river we finally reached Westport, Missouri, near where Kansas City now stands. We arrived there on Sunday, October 23, 1864, just as a big battle was being fought between the Union army under General Alfred Pleasanton and the Confederate army under General Sterling Price. We could hear the roar and boom of the cannon and see the clouds of smoke rising in the sky. Dan and I would have enlisted on the spot had we not been too young. But the smoke of battle got into our nostrils, and we were more determined than ever to reach the far west and fight Indians.

Proceeding northwest, we crossed the Kaw River and found ourselves in Kansas. At that time there were a few warehouses along the banks of the Missouri River where the Kansas City stock yards are now situated. We halted a day or two at the little town of Wyandotte. I remember how the surrounding county was filled with mink, racoon, rabbits, opossums, squirrels, quail and prairie chickens. This was greatly to our liking, so Dan and I hired to an old farmer near Wyandotte, and remained with him a couple of months.

The first signs of spring were now in the air, and like the wild geese that were passing northward, we resumed our migration. At the end of many weary miles we reached Leavenworth, Kansas, and after forming the acquaintance of an old plainsman named Tom Hare, fire and brimstone could not have turned us back, so determined did we become to plunge deep into the wild country that lay beyond us. Hare was a driver in a Government bull train.

I drifted into town hungry and foot-sore, and I will never forget this old man's kindness. He took us to a railroad mess house—the Kansas Pacific grading camp was then at Leavenworth—and gave us our breakfast. While we were eating the old man watched us attentively and seemed pleased with our appearance. In a moment he was telling us of some of his trips in the west, which was like setting out fire in dry stubble. He said that the outfit or bull train to which he belonged was in camp about four miles from town. It was in need of hands, and if we wanted to go on the next trip he would help us get employment, advising us to remain with him until the bull train was ready to start. The outfit was waiting for winter to break up.

We immediately became the old man's staunch friends and ardent admirers. We went out to the camp and when we were taken to the boss, he eyed us carefully and said: "You boys are pretty young, and Bill looks like he ought to be at home with his mother, but I'll give you a chance." So he hired us then and there at $50 a month, with everything furnished, including guns and ammunition. Dan and I were immensely proud of ourselves, and looked forward to the journey with eager expectancy. I was only fourteen years old, but I was delighted with the prospect that at last I should begin the journey across the Plains.

We got orders about April 15 to pull out for Fort Scott, Kansas. We moved by easy marches and reported to the quartermaster when we reached Fort Scott. He ordered the outfit to go into camp a few miles from town on a small stream where there was good grass and water for the stock. There we were to await further orders. We were in camp for two weeks, and all we had to do was to look after the stock, which we did in turns. The stream abounded in fish, and everywhere there were lots of small game. These were among the happiest days of my life. Because of my youth, the men favored me in many ways. I hunted and fished to my heart's content.

I was disappointed that the bull train had been sent south instead of west, but still hoped the order would soon come for us to move toward the Plains. This was in April, 1865, and in southern Kansas the news of President Lincoln's assassination had just been received. I recall that on our way to Fort Scott a black flag of mourning hung on every settler's farmhouse.

One morning about the first of May there was shouting among the men, with the rattling of chains, the creaking of heavy wagons, and the lowing of oxen, as we assembled under orders to proceed to Fort Leavenworth. We moved away in high spirits across the beautiful country, bright and fragrant with the wild flowers of spring. Lawrence was the first town of importance that we reached.

It was the custom of the bull-whackers to make a lively demonstration whenever they passed through a town. With their big sixteen-foot whips they could make a sound like the crack of a rifle, and as rapidly as possible the whips were cracked, the drivers shouting to their oxen, while men, women and children ran into the street to witness the spectacle. It was a performance that everybody thoroughly enjoyed and that never again will be seen in this western country.

In two days from Lawrence we came to Leavenworth City, about three or four miles south of Fort Leavenworth. Here we made the same uproar. Liquor was more plentiful than water at Leavenworth in those days, and many of the bull-whackers "tanked up." There was a big noise all the way to the fort.

Between Lawrence and Leavenworth the country was well settled, and every farmyard was filled with chickens, turkeys, ducks and geese, many of which disappeared about the time we passed that way. Of course I would not be willing to admit that I helped steal any of them, but it would be useless for me to say that I did not help eat from many a well-filled pot. A fat pig that strayed near our camp rarely ever got back home. It is but just to say, however, that this taking of private property was done largely in a spirit of mischief, as these rough bull-whackers could not have been induced to engage in what would have been regarded as actual stealing.

This outfit was made up of men of various ages and occupations. Some had been soldiers, and several had been sailors. I reveled in the stories told by the old gray haired men. I believe that I liked best of all their stories about fighting Indians.

Like all frontier towns, Leavenworth City was well supplied with saloons. It is not surprising that in the West most men drank, as the saloon was the main starting place for an outfit like ours, and a man who did not take at least one drink was considered unfriendly. I wish to emphasize this last word, for my statement is literally true. Inviting a man to drink was about the only way civility could be shown, and to refuse an invitation bordered upon an insult. Again, the saloon was the place where all trails crossed, and there we might be sure of meeting men from the north, from the west and the south, and gaining information that was so essential to those who were journeying into far off places.

The outfit was ordered into camp near the fort, with everybody planning for the westward trip. Our chagrin and disappointment may be imagined when we learned that the whole train was to be sold by the Government, to which it belonged. The country was now green with growing grass, and the cattle were getting sleek and fat. The orderly came and told us to assemble the train in front of the quartermaster's office. The wagons were strung out one after the other until they formed a line half a mile in length. An auctioneer stood in front of the building and cried the sale; as soon as one wagon and team was sold another took its place. The teams were bought in at from $1600 to $1800 each, wagons included, and the twenty-five wagons and three hundred bulls were bought by one man; his name was Kirkendall. He had been master of transportation at Fort Leavenworth. Kirkendall hired our trainmaster, and he in turn hired all the men who wanted to remain with the outfit. About half the men quit, and their

places were filled by fresh bull-whackers. Some of
the latter had never seen a bull train, and had lots
to learn.

By this time I had begun feeling that I was an
old hand. When I was first employed I found it
difficult to yoke my oxen, but my small size appealed to the men, and there was always somebody
willing to help me. I was now able to yoke my
own oxen.

We lay in camp wondering where Kirkendall
would send us. In a few days orders came for us
to pull out for Fort Collins, Colorado, with government supplies. I bubbled over with joy, for
now I was headed for the Plains. Kirkendall received twenty-five cents a pound for the freight he
took out. Each wagon was loaded with about
7,000 pounds of freight, consisting of flour, bacon,
sugar, coffee, ammunition, etc. This outfit was
made up of twenty-five teamsters, one wagon
master, one assistant wagon master, one night
herder, and one extra man to take the place of
any man that might fall sick. Each man was provided with a gun and ammunition.

Before hiring to Kirkendall, we had been paid
off, and I had more money than I had ever
dreamed I would possess at one time. According
to the custom of the country, and not without some
inclination and vanity of my own, I began invest-
ing in good clothes, notably a big sombrero, a Colt's
revolver, a butcher knife, a belt, and a bull whip.
For the latter I paid $7. His whip was the bull-

whacker's pride, and around it circled all his ambition and prowess. Dan bought a similar outfit. I doubt if two boys ever felt more important. I am sure that the older men must have smiled at the two youngsters, each buried beneath his big hat and leaning to one side under the weight of his "shooting irons." How impatient we were for the start! The days seemed to stretch into months. At last, however, we were ready, and whooping farewells, we pulled out.

Little did we dream of the hardships ahead of us. In the comfort of our winter camp we had seen ourselves traveling across the Plains in the bright sunshine of spring, the grass green, the birds singing, and the streams flashing along the way. The winter rains and frosts had made the roads miry and seemingly without bottom. Yet we got along without serious trouble until we reached Salt Creek valley. Here we had to pass through a long lane where the mud was hub deep. We did not realize how bad it was until we were well into the lane. Often we were compelled to put twenty-four oxen to one wagon to pull through some of the bad places. This valley was three or four miles wide, and it took us all day to get across. A man's patience was thoroughly tried, and that day I heard more different kinds of swearing than could be put into a dictionary. After getting out we laid over all next day resting and making repairs. One wagon was sent back to Leavenworth City for material to repair things that had been broken. In

Buffalo as They Looked in the Old Days

Salt Creek valley was pointed out to me a small road house that was said to have been Buffalo Bill's old home.

The road grew better in the neighborhood of Marysville, Kansas, on the Big Blue, where there were a good many settlers. We were making between eight and ten miles a day. The Big Blue is a swift stream, and at the time was in flood, which caused us much trouble in crossing, as cattle do not take well to water, especially when pulling loaded wagons. We doubled our teams, cracked our whips, and forced the reluctant oxen into the torrent with a man on horseback swimming on each side of them, and in this way they swam and struggled to the farther shore. Often the oxen were in danger of drowning, but the whole outfit was crossed without the loss of a single animal.

At this crossing the river made a bend, and the road took the direction of what was called the "dry" route. So we filled our canteens with water and left the river about three o'clock in the afternoon, driving until late that night, and making a dry camp. Next day brought us to the Little Blue, a tributary of the Big Blue. From there our route bore more to the north, going upstream, and in about three days we were in sight of Fort Kearney, Nebraska, and from there, by making a long drive, we got to the Platte River in one day.

All the while since leaving Fort Leavenworth I had been tense with the expectation of seeing a war party of painted Indians, or a herd of buffaloes sweeping over the Plains. Neither had come to pass, and I was keenly disappointed.

When we got to the Platte, we struck a main traveled road leading out from Omaha, Nebraska, St. Joseph, Missouri, and Atchison, Kansas. These three towns were the main shipping points on the Missouri River at that time. Here we could see trains moving along or in camp on the road. Our route led straight up the valley, and in two days we reached a stage station called Plum Creek, where in later years hostile Indians committed many depredations. There seemed to be something in the very air at Plum Creek that was different from what we had left behind. A feeling of danger, invisible but present, was openly manifested when an escort of United States soldiers moved out ahead of us when the bull train started.

This meant that we were in a dangerous locality. In my boyish enthusiasm I was delighted instead of being fearful, for it looked as if we were going into the enemies' country, and from all indications we were, for we could see where the Indians had raided the settlements the previous year. At different places where there had been a road ranch or a small store, their ruins told the tale of fire and rapine by savage Indians. These buildings were built mostly of sod, as there was no timber in the country. Here and there we passed a grave at the side of the road. The raiding had been done by the Cheyennes and Sioux. Practically the only buildings in this part of the country were the relay stations and road ranches of the overland stage company which ran from the Missouri River to California.

After leaving Julesburg, Colorado, the country became much wilder. We saw great herds of antelope and many deer. I was impatient for the sight of buffaloes, and it seemed strange to me that none had appeared. As a matter of fact they had not worked that far north, but were coming later. All along the road after we got on the overland stage route, the stage drivers, who always drove in a gallop as they passed us, would cry out "Indians on ahead! Better look out!" This we found was done jokingly, to alarm such tenderfeet as might be among us, and we soon paid no attention to it, when we encountered no Indians.

Julesburg consisted of a couple of stores and two or three saloons. Here we got a fresh escort of soldiers. Between Plum Creek and Julesburg we passed a big square stone on which was inscribed "Daniel Boone" and other inscriptions, one saying that further information could be found on the other side, meaning the bottom. This stone was so big that twelve men could not move it. We saw where teams had been hitched to it and the stone overturned. We did the same thing, and found the same inscription on the bottom. I doubt if ever a bull train passed that way without turning that big boulder to satisfy its curiosity.

Three days out from Julesburg we left the Platte, and struck a trail called the dry route, at what was known as Freemont's Orchard. There was no sign of an orchard, however. The South Platte had to be forded, and it was a different stream from any we had crossed. We stood in dread of it, as the current was swift and its shores rocky. It took us a whole day to get over, and some wagons had to be partly unloaded.

There were only three horses in the outfit, used by the wagon master, his assistant, and the night herder. They were a great help to us in crossing these streams, as the cattle would follow the horses when no amount of whipping could make them take a bad place. Traveling north, we came to the Cache la Poudre, a beautiful mountain stream in Colorado, beyond which was Fort Collins, which we reached in August, having been on the road two and one-half months.

I now saw mountains for the first time. Fort Collins was situated on the Cache la Poudre in the foothills. Long before we got there they seemed to hang in the sky like clouds. The population of Fort Collins was mostly post traders and soldiers. We remained there about a week, unloading supplies and resting the stock. While there I visited an Indian camp and saw my first Indians. They were Utes, and greatly interested me. The squaws were drying wild cherries for winter, pounding them in a stone mortar. The day before we left Fort Collins a fight took place in our camp between two bull-whackers, Edward Ray and Jim

Lynch, over a game of cards. Ray shot Lynch, and the latter was left in the hospital at Fort Collins.

Our trip back to Fort Leavenworth was over the same route. My journey had fascinated me, but I was disappointed in not having engaged in a fight with Indians, and in not having seen a single buffalo. Going back we were trailing three or four wagons together, and drove the rest of the oxen, taking turns with the teams.

Between Julesburg and Plum Creek we met a party of women on their way to Salt Lake City, Utah, to join the Mormons. There was not a man among them, and they could not speak a word of English; I was told that they were Danes. All the women wore wooden shoes. They drove ox-wagons and had the appearance of being very poor. The sight of these women so excited our curiosity that the trainmaster called a halt until they passed us. Their camp was not a great distance from ours, and that night some of the boys wanted to go and pay them a visit, but the trainmaster told them that if they did not want to get left they had better not go.

There were small stores or road ranches, as they were called, all along the route, generally every ten miles, and often we bought at our own expense such luxuries as sweetmeats and canned goods, which were not to be found in our commissary. Tomatoes sold at fifty cents a can, and everything else was in proportion. When we got back as far as Marysville we could buy fresh vegetables and eggs and chickens by paying a big price for them; but in those days no price was too great to be paid by hungry men. Money was plentiful and if we could get what we wanted, we bought it, regardless of what it cost.

As we approached Leavenworth City, we were met by men soliciting trade for the hotels, stores and saloons, who came out eight or ten miles to meet us. At the fort our wagons were parked, or formed in a square, to be left there for the winter, and the oxen were taken to the country to be fed. By the time we were ready to break camp, hacks and wagons were coming out to take us down town, each business house being represented. We had drawn practically none of our wages during the trip, and when we were paid, many of us felt rich, and had enough to carry us through the winter if we were not extravagant.

November had arrived and the weather was getting cold. There are few sights more chilling and somber than the Plains in winter, stretching brown and dead under a leaden sky, with the wind moaning and roaring from the north. We could have found jobs with other outfits, as trains were being fitted out for western forts, to both Fort Lyon and Fort Riley. Dan and I would have gone as bull-whackers with these, but were advised by older men not to go, as it would be a hard trip in winter storms and blizzards. Dan and I remained together for a week, enjoying the sights. He decided to go back to his old home in Indiana, where he could be with his old friends during the winter. Strangely, I never afterward heard of or saw him.

In returning from Fort Collins, I had become strongly attached to another young fellow named Johnny Baldwin. We were together in the street one day when we met up with the master of a bull-train that was getting ready to start to Fort Larned. He was a gruff old codger, and looked as rusty as a six-shooter that had lain all winter in the snow. He asked us to go with him, and we would have gone if we had not struck a better job that very day. After we had told him that we would decide by next day, we wandered into the street. There we met a man who caught our fancy beyond all others we had seen. He was a jolly, good-natured fellow who joked with us and said that he would like to hire us to go with a government mule train that was outfitting. He said that we would get to see "lots of corn-fed country girls" out in the country where the mules were being fed for the winter. He offered us each $45 a month, and we hired to him on the spot.

This proved to be a much easier job than the one we had just left. The outfit consisted of about 150 head of mules that had been driven to a farm on Soldiers' Creek, about sixty miles from Leavenworth, near where Holton, Kas., now stands. Here we remained all winter. About all

I had to do was to help the cook and round in the mules at night. We had an abundance of good things to eat, and grew fat and "sassy."

When the men discovered that I was a good shot, I was given a job that was wholly to my liking—hunting game for the mess. There were plenty of quails, rabbits, squirrels and prairie chickens, and I was in my glory. I ranged the country, a youthful Daniel Boone, enjoying every moment of the time. I seemed to have a natural aptitude in the handling of fire-arms. It was my greatest ambition to become a good shot. In later years I was counted an expert marksman in any company, regardless of how proficient my rivals might be. I always attributed my skill with the rifle to my natural love for the sport, to steady nerves, and to constant, unremitting practice. Where other men found pleasure in cards, horse-racing and other similar amusements, I was happiest when ranging the open country with my gun on my shoulder and a dog at my heels, far out among the wild birds and the wild animals.

In the neighborhood of our camp were a good many settlers, sturdy, strong people, who lived in the style of the frontier, and, I dare say, got much more contentment out of life than many who came after them and lived under more civilized conditions. During the winter, dances and parties were frequent, and we were hospitably invited to attend them. I went with the men, but was entirely too bashful to take part. I sat beside the fiddlers and looked at the pretty girls, rosy and blushing, and would have given a fortune—had I possessed one—for courage enough to walk boldly up to the handsomest, ask her to dance with me, and then to dance without making blunders as the figures were called. Alas, such courage and assurance were quite beyond my strongest resolves. I remember, particularly, one black-eyed girl who observed my embarrassment, and would always speak to me and invite me to take part. I adored her for this, but would have fled like an antelope had she approached me.

Along about the first of March we got orders to take the mules to Leavenworth. We were elated at the prospect of change. Where were we going? How long would we be gone? What would be our adventures? These were questions that came to us thick and fast. This was one of the splendid things of life in frontier days—this eagerness to be off and away after a season of hibernation. Many a hunter, many a scout, many a cowboy, returning from a long and arduous expedition, would swear that never again would he endure misery and hardships such as he had encountered. All winter he would stay close to the cook and roast his shins beside the fire, dead sure that he was forever done with the roving life. Then, one day, came the honking of wild geese flying northward; the sun grew warmer; the grass was springing green around the buffalo chips on the prairie, and in the draws the redbud was lifting itself in little pink clouds. Farewell to all firm resolves! A yoke of oxen could not have held the plainsman in the quarters which he had believed to be the most delightful place in the world, when he arrived there in the fall. Something was calling him—something in the wind, the sky and the dashing rain—and he went, went like a bird from its cage.

The day we broke camp a "norther" began blowing, and I froze two of my fingers rather badly. We traveled thirty-five or forty miles the first day, the mules going at a gallop part of the time. We reached Fort Leavenworth next day, and delivered our mules to the corral-master, after which we went to the Government mess house, where our appetites attracted considerable attention and caused no less comment.

The quartermaster paid us our accumulated wages. We were now without a job. A friendship had grown up between myself and a man named Bill Gladden. The two of us went from the Fort to the city, and remained there about three weeks, attracted by the curious sights to be seen daily in the coming and going of the multitudes of brawny men who gave to that town a historic interest.

The manager of the farm where I had spent the winter was named McCall. His family seemed to feel much affection for me. His son, Charley, and I became fast friends. McCall offered me a job, which Gladden advised me to accept, as he felt that I was rather young to be fighting my way against the odds that often overthrew strong men in the Plains Country. This, however, was not what I wanted to do. I had made up my mind to go west—and to keep on going west until I could say that I had seen it all, and had hunted buffaloes and fought Indians to my complete satisfaction. Little did I dream of how much of this sort of thing was in store for me in later years. The McCalls were so persuasive however, that I could not resist their kind offers, and I remained on the farm about a year. During all this time Mrs. McCall was a mother to me, and the family treated me as if I were a son and a brother. I am sure that the good influences of this home were helpful to me in after life.

I worked for the McCalls until the fall of 1866. In July a number of horses were stolen from the barn, and my employer gave me the place of night watchman, a responsible position for a boy of my age. I had the greatest confidence, however, in my ability to use my rifle in a way that would be disastrous to thieves. I did not lose a single horse.

The McCalls had two girls and one boy, Charley. The latter was wild and reckless, but good-hearted and eager for any kind of adventure. Once he had run away from home and gone west with a Government mule train. Old man McCall was a great hand to hunt, and often took me with him on his hunting trips. I always thought that he felt a bit provoked at me when his folks teased him about my killing the most game, but he laughed it off, and would brag on me himself.

That fall the McCalls told me that if I wished to remain and go to school during the winter, my board would not cost me a cent. I was glad to take advantage of this offer, so Charley and I walked to town every day to school—the two girls attended a Catholic school. Prior to this, I had attended school only two terms. Plainly, my school days were limited.

I did my best to keep Charley out of trouble, and am sure that I exerted a good influence over him, as he would nearly always listen to me. Despite my utmost endeavors, he engaged in a number of fights at school, which caused his parents more or less trouble. During all our acquaintance Charley and I never spoke a harsh word to each other.

While I was living with the McCalls a shocking tragedy took place at their home—the suicide of United States Senator James Lane, of Kansas. He was visiting there at the time he killed himself. Mrs. Lane and Mrs. McCall were sisters. The Senator was in poor health. While riding with his wife and children, he thrust the muzzle of a six-shooter into his mouth, and pulled the trigger. The bullet came out at the top of his head. Strange to say, he lived three days. I was with the ambulance that was sent out to convey him to Leavenworth, where he could receive medical aid. Senator Lane was a Kansas pioneer, and took an active and leading part in the conduct of its early affairs.

Leavenworth City was a tough place in those days, filled with all kinds of rough characters. I saw three men lying dead in the street one day, as the result of an extraordinary occurrence. Four men were sitting under a tree playing cards, as a severe electric storm formed and swept over the city. One man suggested that the game should be postponed until after the storm had passed, to which another replied, "D——n the lightning." At that moment a bolt struck the tree with a blinding flash, killing all of the men save the one that had asked that there be no card-playing while the storm was raging. The bodies of the dead men were laid on the floor of the fire station. Their deaths caused much comment, as many persons felt that they had provoked the wrath that fell upon them.

Shootings were as common as the arrival of a bull-train, and excited little comment. The man who was quickest on the trigger usually came out ahead—the other fellow was buried, and no questions asked.

CHAPTER III

WHEN the spring of 1867 came around I was offered my old job on the farm, and Mrs. McCall, a kind, good woman, used all her influence to get me to accept it. But my head was filled with dreams of adventure in the Far West. Always, I could see the West holding its hands toward me, and beckoning and smiling.

Meeting a Government trainmaster named Simpson, who was hiring men to go out with a train that was to be shipped by railroad as far as Fort Harker, I forgot all that Mrs. McCall had said to me about staying on the farm, and hired to Simpson. Returning to the farm, I told my good friends good-bye.

The Kansas Pacific railroad had now been built as far west as Fort Harker. All our wagons and harness were new and these, together with the mules, were loaded into cars and shipped to Fort Harker. We went into camp close to the Fort.

In this outfit were a good many raw men, while the mules were known as "shave-tails," which meant wild, unbroken mules; only a few had been harnessed and driven. By this time I could handle a team with as much ease as a man could. In my lot were two or three gentle mules—I have cause to remember one old fellow in particular, upon whose back I afterwards had one of the most exciting rides of my life.

We put in ten days breaking the "shave-tails." It was a scene of hilarious excitement, and not without danger, as often mules would be kicking and bucking in harness with might and main, while others would be running away. At such times the drivers had no chance to pay attention to other things.

While in this camp, cholera began raging at Fort Harker, which struck terror to many who stood in no fear of other dangers to life. Many of our men deserted, and two died of the dread disease. I witnessed the death of one of our men, Frinkum, and shall never forget his agony. Men who were apparently in the full vigor of health at sunrise lay dead by night. The authorities kept the number of dead secret as much as possible. The burials were usually at night.

This epidemic of death extended from Fort Harker, Kansas, to Fort Union, New Mexico. Its origin was said to have been in the Tenth Cavalry, a negro command, which had shipped from the East to the western frontier. Now, all this excitement did not bother me a bit—I did not think much about it. The doctors made regular calls at our camp every day, and we were placed on a strict diet. We were forbidden to eat any kind of vegetable or fresh meat. The disease ran its course in about three weeks.

Alas, and again alas, up to this time I had never seen a buffalo! I could almost taste buffalo, so keen was I to behold one of these shaggy monsters, pawing the sandy plain, throwing dust high in air, and shaking his ponderous head at his enemies, defying them to battle.

The Government here issued a new lot of arms and ammunition to us. This looked warlike, and was greatly to my liking. The guns were the Sharpe's carbines, each carrying a linen cartridge, with which was used the "army hat" cap. In addition, we were given a six-shooting Remington cap and ball pistol. These were the very latest arms.

Now came an eventful, a momentous morning. I had just crawled from under my blankets and was feeding my mules. Glancing to the northwest, I saw a lone object on the plains. At the moment the object apparently failed to make an impression upon my mind, and I turned toward my mules. Then I jumped as if I had been stung by a hornet. With eyes distended, I whirled and looked again at the lone object on the Plains. My body was vibrating as if touched by a dynamo.

A buffalo! No mistake about it. There he stood, rather far off and dim. Maybe he had been waiting for me all these years, waiting for me to see him. That was my buffalo. I determined that I should get him, even if I had to twist my fingers in his shaggy mane and drag him alive into camp.

Seizing a blind-bridle. I slipped it onto the

gentle old mule to which I referred in an earlier page, made a dash for my rifle, and rode away bareback and at top speed after the buffalo.

The buffalo had turned and was moving away from camp when he caught sight of the boy on the mule riding wildly toward him. With a flip of his tail, the buffalo struck his rocking-chair gait and went lumbering away. Up and down hills and across gullies he galloped. I was hot behind him, and at times was just at the point of getting range only to see the buffalo increase his speed and spoil my shot.

We had consumed about four miles in this sort of thing, when we came to a smooth flat. My old mule was panting and pretty well winded by this time, but I was able to make him take another spurt in speed. This brought me within range. The buffalo fell dead at the first shot. The explosion scared the mule into hysteria, but his was no worse than mine. I had not only killed a buffalo, but had killed, unaided, the first buffalo I ever saw.

By this time three or four men from the outfit had arrived. They were jubilant over my success, and were kind enough to exaggerate the distance of the shot. The buffalo was a hard animal to kill instantly, as a vital spot had to be struck. We skinned the carcass, and each man cut off a chunk of meat and took it back to camp. Greatly to our disgust, not a mouthful were we allowed to cook or eat, because of the cholera quarantine.

A few days later orders were given to load the wagons with Government supplies for Fort Hays, Kansas, ninety odd miles west of Fort Harker. By this time our "shave-tail" mules were under fairly good control, and we got under headway without much trouble.

On this trip, at a distance, we saw a bunch of Indian warriors, but did not come in contact with them. In my lack of experience I was eager for the fray, and was disappointed when I saw the war party disappear over a long ridge, without my having been able to test my marksmanship and my new Sharpe's rifle. Buffaloes were seen in numbers, and I was lucky enough to kill several "on my own hook." We reached Fort Hays in about four days, and returned to Fort Harker in about the same time.

Fort Hays was garrisoned mostly by negro soldiers. No buildings had been erected at that time, and we unloaded our supplies in the open prairie, where guards had been stationed to protect them. The timber for the buildings was being hauled from Fort Harker.

Our next trip was to Fort Wallace, with Government supplies, the distance being considerably greater than from Fort Harker to Fort Hays. We always had an escort of soldiers, as there was constant danger of meeting an Indian war party.

In August, 1867, we were sent to Fort Lyon, and on this trip we saw thousands of buffaloes. The breeding season was now approaching its close, and at night and early morning could be heard the constant, low thunder of the bulls, their grunting rising into a roar that was one of the most striking of the natural phenomena of the Plains country. The calves, by this time, were alert, active little fellows, closely guarded by their mothers. Later in the season, all the bulls would segregate themselves from the cows, to range apart until the next breeding season. West of Fort Dodge we saw Indians in war paint, and expected to be attacked, but the rascals veered round us and went on their way.

Fort Hays was on a tributary of the Smoky Hill River; old Fort Zarah, on Walnut Creek; Fort Larned, on Pawnee Fork; and Fort Harker, on Big Creek. All these forts were being remodeled and improved. In this way we put in all that summer, hauling supplies to one fort or the other, and when not engaged in this, we hauled rock for the foundations of the buildings.

Early in the autumn, 1867, while several Government trains were at Fort Harker, waiting for orders, we were notified to make ready to accompany a party of peace commissioners that had been authorized to treat with several of the main Plains tribes of Indians in the Southwest, at Medicine Lodge, Kas. These negotiations resulted in what were afterwards known as the Medicine Lodge Treaties. Like most other treaties with these tribes, they were soon broken.

Several trains, with a part of ours, were to accompany this expedition. I was eager to go, but as no orders had been given to my outfit, I was fearful that I might be left behind. Here was the opportunity I had long looked for—to see a big gathering of Indians close at hand, without danger of getting scalped. I had almost given up in despair, when an orderly galloped up from headquarters, saying that two more wagons must be sent forward at once. It was now 6 o'clock in the evening. Simpson, our wagon-master, approached me and said:

"Billy, you and Frickie (Frickie drove the wagon next to mine) get ready at once and go into Fort Harker."

As a rule, nothing ever greatly excited me in my frontier days, but I am bound to admit that I was now going round and round, so overjoyed was I at my good luck. My agitation came near causing me to be left behind.

I ran as quickly as possible to where my mules were eating their grain, and without halting jerked the harness from the rack to throw it onto the lead mule. With both feet this mule kicked me squarely in the small of the back. I dropped as if I had been struck with an axe, and found myself partly paralyzed, and scarcely able to move. Recovering slightly, I regained my feet, but found that I could not straighten my body. I was game, however. Calling Frickie, I told him what had happened, and asked him to help me harness my mules, and not to say a word to anybody about my being hurt. Were it known that I had been kicked, I might be sent to the hospital. Frickie was a good fellow, and I was soon on my way to the Fort. By next morning I was in fairly good shape.

Night had come by the time we reached Fort Harker. We had to load and then drive about three miles to camp, on the Smoky Hill. The last two wagons were loaded with ammunition for a small Gatling gun, not an undesirable equipment on Indian peace expeditions in those days.

We pulled out bright and early next morning for Plum Creek, where there was a small road-ranch. Next day we reached Fort Zarah on Walnut Creek and on the third day we went on up the Arkansas and crossed it about seven miles below Fort Larned. We reached Medicine Lodge on the fourth day, where the council was to be held.

All along the way on this trip we were traveling through countless numbers of buffaloes. I remember seeing a wounded buffalo cow followed by six big lobo wolves. No hoofed animal could withstand these savage beasts—they were a terror to other wild life on the Plains. Wantonly, several buffaloes had been shot, and left lying to rot on the ground. An orderly came riding down the line with strict orders, that if another man in the outfit fired another shot at a buffalo he would be placed in irons.

Between the Arkansas River and Medicine Lodge we were met by a number of noted Indian chiefs, mounted upon their finest horses and arrayed in their most splendid costumes. They carried themselves with dignity and in every feature was revealed their racial pride and their haughty contempt of the white man.

Satank, chief of the Kiowas, rode a big black horse and presented a magnificent appearance. It was because of his complaint that the order had been issued against the killing of buffaloes—a complaint that lay at the very heart of the grievances of the Indian against the white man in frontier days. He declared that the buffalo were the property of himself and his people, and to destroy the buffalo meant the destruction of the Indian. Leading a nomadic life, which prevented his tilling the soil, even if he had wished to engage in agriculture, which he did not, the Indian saw that he would be deprived of his principal and most necessary food—buffalo meat—if the buffalo were killed.

At a later day General Phil Sheridan, to subdue and conquer the Plains tribes for all time, urged and practiced the very thing that Satank was fearful might happen. In the early 70's, the state legislatures of Kansas and Colorado, listening to the appeal of the Indians, through sympathetic white persons, enacted laws to stop the slaughtering of the buffalo. General Sheridan at that time was in command of the Military Department of the Southwest, with headquarters at San Antonio. The Texas legislature, in session

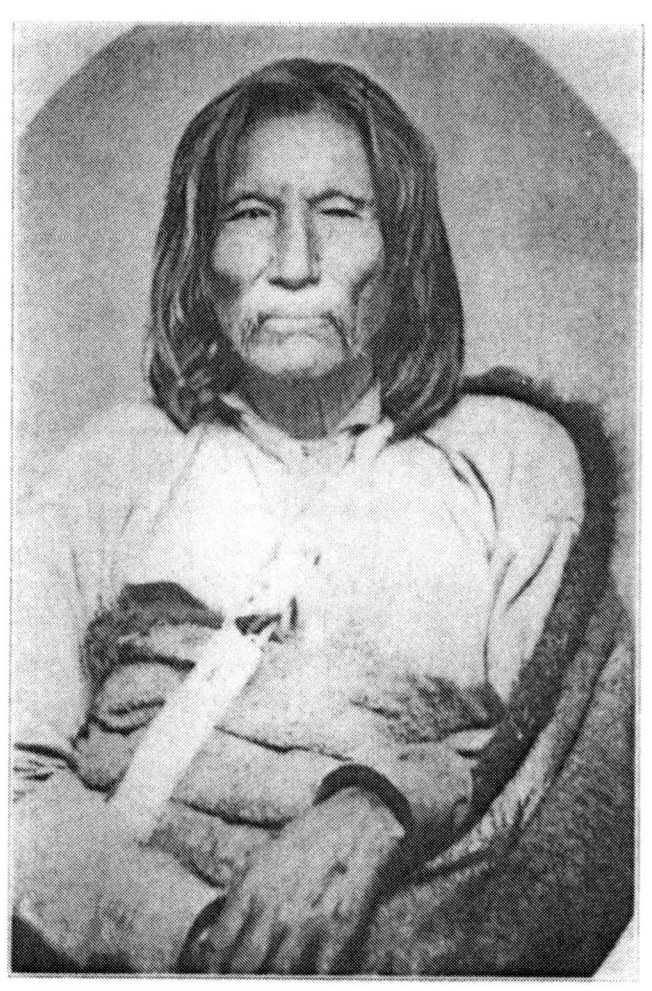

SATANK, THE OLD TIGER OF THE KIOWAS

at Austin, was at the point of declaring against the merciless slaughter of buffalo that was then under way in the Staked Plains and Panhandle regions. General Sheridan is said to have told the legislators that the state should give to every buffalo-hunter a bronze medal, on one side of which should be a dead buffalo, and on the other, a discouraged Indian, adding:

"These men have done more in the last year to settle the vexed Indian question than the entire regular army has done in the last thirty years. They are destroying the Indians' commissary; and it is a well-known fact that an army losing its base of supplies is placed at a great disadvantage. Send them powder and lead, if you will; but, for the sake of a lasting peace, let them kill, skin, and sell until the buffaloes are exterminated. Then your prairies can be covered with speckled cattle, and the festive cowboy, who follows the hunter as a second fore-runner of an advanced civilization."

The Texas legislature accepted General Sheridan's advice. The Texans as a people were readily disposed to agree with that point of view, for in no State did the Plains Indians commit crimes more cruel and horrible than in Texas.

On our way to Medicine Lodge our train of several hundred wagons was strung out for a distance of about two miles, accompanied by a strong escort of soldiers.

The members of this Indian Peace Commission were: N. G. Taylor, Commissioner of Indian

Affairs; John B. Henderson, United States
Senator; General William Tecumseh Sherman;
General W. H. Harney; General John B. San-
born; General A. H. Terry; Colonel S. F. Tap-
pan, and General C. C. Augur.

Among the notable chiefs were: Satanta, Kicking Bird, Black Kettle, Medicine Arrow, and
Lone Wolf. Black Kettle was then at the height
of his power, but soon to meet a tragic and unde-
served death. He had been in the Sand Creek fight
in Colorado, November, 1864, where Colonel Chivington, commanding a regiment of Colorado
troops, massacred a lot of friendly Cheyennes. I
camped on that battleground in 1870 while hunting buffalo. The spot was still strewn with bones
of the dead, and the trees were yet scarred by the
hail of bullets that had come from the guns of the
soldiers, who killed old and young, women and
children, without mercy, and atrociously mutilated the bodies of the dead. In 1866, at Fort
Harker, Black Kettle had made a speech of great
eloquence, asking the Government not to permit
the building of railroads through the Indian
country, as it would drive away the buffalo and
leave the Indians to starve.

This fear of the change that would follow the
building of railroads across the Plains was night
and day in the heart of the Indian. No chief
made a speech in which he did not refer to it. In
June, 1871, Little Raven, Powder Face, and
Bird Chief, Arapahoes; Little Robe and Stone

Calf, Cheyennes, and Buffalo Good, Wichita, were taken to Washington and Boston, that they might be impressed with the white man's strength, and the futility of the Indians' further resistance to the demands of the Government. Stone Calf, in a speech at Tremont Temple, Boston, handled the railroad question in this manner.

"'They (the Government) said they would teach our people to plant and raise corn, and to build our habitations from trees. But before they ever ploughed or planted an acre of corn for us they commenced to build railroads through our country. What use have we for railroads in our country? What have we to transport from our nations? Nothing. We are living wild, really living on the prairies as we have in former times. I do not see that we have been benefited in the least by all the treaties that we have made with the United States Government."

We went into camp on Medicine Lodge Creek, to wait until the gathering Indians had come in. Near us was a small village of Indians, to whom a runner came on the third day to notify them that some of their livestock had been stolen by the Kaws, a neighboring tribe. We could see the wave of excitement run over the village, and the bucks running to and fro, getting ready for the pursuit. The squaws were no less active. They helped saddle the ponies, etc., and jabbered and screamed to each other in a way that would have made it hard for the marauders had they been captives in the custody of the squaws. As each buck got ready, he rode away without waiting for his companions. They returned later in the day with their ponies, but had been unable to overtake the thieves.

I shall never forget the morning of October 28, 1867. At a distance of about two miles from our camp was the crest of a low swell in the Plains. The background was blue sky—a blue curtain that touched the brown Plains. For a moment I was dumbfounded at sight of what was rising over that crest and flowing with vivid commotion toward us. It was a glittering, fluttering, gaily colored mass of barbarism, the flower and perfection of the war strength of the Plains Indian tribes. The resplendent warriors, armed with all their equipment and adorned with all the regalia of battle, seemed to be rising out of the earth. Their number was estimated at 1500, but I cannot vouch for its accuracy.

As they came into plainer view, the Indians spread their ranks wider and wider, to create as profound an impression as possible, and inspire us deeply with their power. Now they could be heard chanting and singing. Having arrived within a quarter of a mile of our camp, the Indians charged like a whirlwind, firing their guns and brandishing them above their heads. The charge was abruptly halted, and the Indians stood at rest, waiting for the negotiations to begin. The tribes represented were the Cheyenne, Arapahoe, Kiowa, Apache, and Comanche.

While the Indians were advancing, and were about half a mile distant, orders were given in camp that every man should retire at once to his tent, and there hold himself in readiness to resist an attack, which might be made at any moment. My boyish curiosity got the better of me, and I was standing just outside the door of my tent, gazing with open mouth at the oncoming Indians. General Harney was walking up and down the line between the tents, encouraging the men, telling them not to be afraid, as we had enough men to whip all the Indians in sight. He saw me as he was passing my tent. Tapping me on the shoulder with his riding whip, he said, "Get back into your tent, young man." I lost no time in obeying him.

This fine old warrior made a lasting impression upon me, and I can see him now, as if it were only yesterday, passing back and forth in the camp street, with the fire of valor burning in his eyes. He felt the responsibility of this critical moment, and knew that the slightest break on either side would precipitate war on the spot. He made an imposing appearance that memorable fall morning. He was gray-haired, straight, broad-shoul-dered, and towered to the commanding height of six feet and six inches. General Harney was an experienced Indian fighter, and exerted a powerful influence among the Plains tribes. They knew him and respected him, believing that he had always told them the truth.

The Indians drew up their horses at a distance of about 200 yards. General Harney had motioned to them to stop, and for their principal chiefs to come into camp. The latter were obedient to his request and after dismounting, sat down with the peace commissioners. At the end of about an hour's conference, the main body of Indians was permitted to enter camp. There were many Indian boys not more than ten years old among the warriors, which probably was an artifice to create among us the belief that there were more fighting men than were actually in the ranks.

Bringing up the rear were the squaws and children and dogs. The squaws pitched their tepees on the creek in sight of our camp.

The young bucks spurned all friendly overtures, refusing to shake hands, and conducting themselves in a sullen manner. After riding through our camp many times, evidently to examine it carefully and gain an accurate knowledge of our strength, they withdrew and remained at a distance. During this time the troops were intently watching every movement of the Indians, suspecting treachery at every turn.

The commission and the chiefs finally agreed upon the terms of the treaties, the main point of which was that the Indians should keep south of the Arkansas River, I had reason to remember this particular provision in subsequent years, as did many another buffalo-hunter. To venture south of the Arkansas for buffalo was to risk falling into the very jaws of the lion, as the Indians fought jealously for the preservation of the right which they declared had been given to them at Medicine Lodge.

The making of treaties with the Plains tribes was followed by the breaking of these treaties whenever the Indians saw fit to do so. Conditions generally made it difficult for the Indians to do otherwise. They were beset on all sides by a frontier population that was as hostile to the Indians as the Indian was to the whites. Lack of permanency and continuity in the arrangements made by the Federal government were largely responsible for the unrest and frequent outbreaks. The situation was clearly described by General W. B. Hazen in 1874, when most of the southwestern tribes had gone on the warpath. He said:

"As one example of this very point, I will call attention to successive treaties made with the Kiowas, Satanta at the head, by five separate and successive commissions, each ignorant of what the other had done, and believing that they alone were receiving the fresh faith of these people. Several solemn treaties were made, by which these people were to cease war, and especially raiding into Texas, previous to the Medicine Lodge treaty of 1867, all to be broken within thirty days thereafter. Then comes that of Medicine Lodge, terms of which you know. Then one was made with General Sheridan and myself, at Fort Larned, in the autumn of 1868, to be quickly broken. Then, again, in 1869, with General Sheridan, to be broken not less than twenty times, until Satanta was imprisoned in Texas. Then a new farce with the commissioners, by which he was released, and he is now leading the war party of the tribe. This would have been impossible had there not been men ignorant of the situation, at each successive occasion to deal with these people, nor could it have taken place had the Army, with its persistent organization, control of Indian affairs. Such is the case all through the administration of Indian matters. One civil administration, or one set of civil officers, in good faith undertakes an experimental policy, good enough of itself, but as soon almost as a plan sets under way a supplanting administration begins, with equally good intent, an entirely new policy, unintentionally disregarding all the promises and efforts of its predecessors and their agents. The savage cannot comprehend this, and naturally calls it a lie, the white people a nation of liars, and as evidence relates a half dozen cases like that just described. I am giving no fictitious imaginings but what I know. This thoroughly destroys any faith or interest that otherwise may be nourished in an Indian community; this can be changed only by giving them a consecutive policy, which is impractical only through some branch of government that is in itself perpetual."

The "peace policy" of the Government actually encouraged a number of the more daring chiefs to become defiant in their dealings with Washington. When they saw that the Government did not strike back, or strike back quickly, they did not hesitate to go on raids and commit depredations. Shortly after Satanta and Big Tree, Kiowas, had been paroled by the Texas authorities, in 1873, the Commissioner of Indian Affairs, then at Fort Sill, demanded the surrender and arrest of certain Comanche warriors who had been raiding in Texas, saying that if this order should not be obeyed within ten days, it would be enforced by military power. A portion of the Comanche warriors immediately left for the Plains, and it being evident that an attempt to compel compliance by military force could be successful only after a long campaign, the order was suspended and no arrests were made.

The effect of this wavering policy was bad. The same hostile warriors of the Comanches and Kiowas considering themselves victorious, became more and more open in their hostile demonstrations, and during the winter and spring frequent consultations were held by them, sometimes including the neighboring Cheyennes, looking to the marauding expeditions upon a larger scale than for the many years before. Some time in May, at the annual "Medicine" dance of the Comanches, near the mouth of the Sweetwater, one of their young men, making his first appearance as a "medicine" man or prophet, professed to have a revelation from the Great Spirit, to the effect that the Caddoes, Wichitas, and other friendly Indians who were following in the way of the whites, would soon go out of existence, and that this would be the fate of the Comanches if they followed the same road; the only way for them to become the great and powerful nation they once were, was to go to war and kill all the white people they could. The Indians said that he had predicted the great drouth of that year; that he had told them the bullets would drop harmlessly from the guns of the white men; that he had appealed to them for the truth of his revelation by predicting that the comet, then attracting general attention, would disappear in five days, and had made other demonstrations which to them appeared miraculous and obtained for him entire credence for all his words. The hearts of all the young Comanche warriors were at once fired. Another "medicine" dance was soon after appointed, to which all Kiowas and Cheyennes were invited, when the Comanche " medicine" man again appeared, and at which plans were discussed and determined on for a campaign of murder and rapine. From this period murders and depredations became so frequent as to excite general alarm.

War parties were soon ranging through what is now western Oklahoma, the Texas Panhandle, western Kansas, and eastern Colorado. The war plans of the Kiowas, Comanches and Cheyennes were consolidated by an exciting occurrence at Wichita Agency, August 22, 1874, which inflamed them to outbreaks on a larger scale.

A number of Kiowas and the Noconee band of Comanches with their squaws and children went to the Agency and began raiding the fields and gardens of the friendly Wichitas. General J. W. Davidson, in command at Fort Sill, was notified, and he sent Lieutenant Woodward with a detail of forty men of the Tenth Cavalry to disarm the hostiles and compel their return to Fort Sill. Big Red Food, the chief, turned over a few guns and pistols, but declared that he would not surrender his bows and arrows. In the latter he was supported by the terms of a recent agreement in which it was held that only guns should be classed as arms. With a whoop Big Red Food and his warriors dashed away. The soldiers fired a volley at the Indians. The latter destroyed much property and committed several murders in the neighborhood of the Agency. The war party quickly grew in numbers, and prospect of peace in the Plains country was vanishing.

Wagon loads of supplies and presents had been brought for the Indians, all of which were now distributed. The supplies were mostly blankets, clothing, hats, sugar, coffee and flour, which were issued to the head men, and these in turn made distribution among the families. The Indians now seemed in much better humor.

The day was warm, though fall was at hand, and

the heat brought much discomfort to some of the Indians—those, for instance, who put on every article of clothing that had been given to them. It was a comical sight to see some of the old bucks wearing two or three heavy coats and two high-crowned Army hats, one on top of the other. Others were attired in Army uniforms, but without trousers. The latter was a garment which no wild Indian could be induced to wear.

In a short time there was much trading going on between the soldiers and the Indians, but on the sly, as strict orders had been issued against it, especially the trading of any kind of fire-arms to the Indians. The temptation was too strong, however, and I traded my old cap-and-ball six-shooter to an old Indian for three buffalo robes and other trinkets.

About 4 o'clock in the afternoon of the day the Indians came in we got orders to be ready to pull out in an hour. It was nearly sundown when we broke camp. We traveled until late that night to reach the Arkansas River crossing, where we went over and made camp.

We pulled into Fort Harker about November 1, and drove on out to where the rest of the train was in camp. While unloading our wagons at the Post, a rumor spread that gave us some uneasiness—a rumor about what might happen to the fellows who traded firearms to the Indians at Medicine Lodge. The fine for a man who had sold a six-shooter would be fifty dollars, which was enough money to buy a whole lot of fun in those days.

These arms were the property of the United States Government, and proof that a man had sold a gun meant serious trouble. An order came to the men to turn in all their arms. It looked as if I was in bad shape. In my predicament Frickie again came to my aid, and just in the nick of time, by offering to lend me his six-shooter—a six-shooter which he personally owned. I turned in Frickie's gun, and later received another, which I gave to him.

We had grown rather tired of the job of telling the boys that had stayed behind all about the Medicine Lodge treaty by the time orders came for us to hitch up for a trip to Fort Leavenworth. At Fort Harker was a lot of artillery that had been assembled there in 1867 by General Hancock for an Indian campaign. He found that dragging cannon here and there over the Plains in pursuit of hostile Indians was about as feasible as hitting a hummingbird with a brickbat. The Indians moved like the wind or like shadows, and were too wary to come within range of artillery. So the cannons were parked at Fort Harker as useless. All of them were to be hauled back by wagon to Fort Leavenworth. Our trail led along the railway for miles, and it seemed ridiculous that the cannons should not be transported by train. The cost of shipment would have been excessive, however, and inasmuch as the government owned the teams and wagons and was paying us by the month there was no good reason why we should not be hauling cannon to Fort Leavenworth.

We made our first camp near Salina, Kas., and narrowly escaped losing our wagons by fire. In the early morning, a spark blew from a camp-fire into the tall, dry grass. Instantly, the fire began running with the speed of a race horse. All hands turned out to save tents, bedding, wagons, etc. By back-firing, and by beating out the flames near our tents, we were able to get the fire under control. At best, however, we should have lost our wagons had it not been for our good luck in having the teams hitched before the fire broke out. This enabled us to shift the position of the wagons as necessity required.

The fires on the Plains in fall and winter, after frost had cured the grass, were often a magnificent spectacle, especially at night when their radiance reddened the sky for many miles. The sky would be luminous, even though the fire was too far beyond the horizon to be seen. Once under strong headway, with the fire spread over a wide area, it was difficult to arrest its progress. To the experienced plainsman, equipped with a flint or matches, there was no imminent danger, as he knew how to set out protective fires, and thus insure his safety.

These big fires were rather terrifying, nevertheless, especially to the "tenderfoot." Carried forward in the teeth of a high, boisterous wind, the fire was appalling, and there was something sinister and somber in the low roar that sent terror to the heart of wild animals. Vast clouds of smoke were carried into the heavens, until the sun lost its radiance and hung red and dull, like a copper shield, in the opaque depths. The ashes of burned vegetation sifted down hour after hour, as if a volcano were throwing out fine lava dust. At night, when the wind was still, a fire on the Plains was a beautiful sight. In the far distance, the tongues of flame appeared so small that they looked like a red line of countless fingers, pointing with trembling motion toward the sky. The danger of these fires to life in the Plains country has been exaggerated. The grass that grew in the Plains did not have the height to produce a sweeping, high-rolling fire, such as was often seen in the regions of the tall bluestem in eastern Kansas.

Upon reaching Fort Leavenworth, the wagons were unloaded, the outfits turned over to the Government, and the "shave-tail drivers" paid off. I had a comfortable stake for a young fellow, and spent the winter in Leavenworth and Kansas City, mingling with the hardy frontiersmen and listening delightedly to their incomparable tales of adventure. I went frequently to the home of my friends, the McCalls, where I always found a hospitable welcome. Several times I went out from both Leavenworth and Kansas City with hunting parties. In those days, railroad companies used to promote "personally conducted" hunting parties to the buffalo range, hunters coming from such distances as Cincinnati, Chicago, and St. Louis.

CHAPTER IV

IN the spring of 1868 I obtained employment with a man named Powers who owned a store at Baxter Springs, Kas. Powers owned a train of six wagons, all drawn by four-mule teams, which he kept on the road hauling lumber and supplies from Leavenworth to Baxter. Much has been written about Dodge City, Caldwell and Abilene as wild and woolly towns in frontier days. None of them was livelier than Baxter Springs, especially after the completion of the railroad to that point. Baxter was the northern terminus of a trail from Texas across the Indian Territory. The Territory was infested by the most desperate class of men I ever saw. Baxter Springs supplied in abundance all that the most dissipated character could wish for in the way of whisky, women, gambling and fighting. The story of the early days at Baxter would make a fascinating book.

At Baxter I saw the battleground where Quantrell, the guerilla, captured General Blunt's supply train in 1864. The capture was virtually a horrible massacre by this blood-thirsty "partisan ranger" and his men. I was told that Quantrell got General Blunt's uniform, and afterwards wore it. I could still see the bullet marks on the trees where the fight took place.

I remained with Powers most of that summer, hauling from Kansas City part of the time. I was still bent upon getting further west. I thirsted for adventure, but as yet had seen only the mere fringe of it. At the end of several months, I went to Leavenworth with a lot of freighters, and there met up with a man named Cox who was hiring men to go with a mule train to Fort Hays. I hired to Cox, as did Sam Harkness, a companion with whom I had worked all summer. To our great satisfaction, we were told that the mules, which had been shipped from Missouri and Kentucky, were all broke and by no means the desperate "shave-tails" that confronted me when I started from Leavenworth for the first time.

These were exciting times. The very air buzzed with news of Indian depredations. The Government was rushing troops and supplies to the front, as if the world were coming to an end. The Indians had broken out again, and were leaving a trail of blood and ashes in the valley of the Solomon, where settlements were in abject terror, not knowing at what moment a swiftly moving war party might descend and murder the inhabitants, burn the buildings and drive off the livestock. Worst of all was the nature of the cruelties inflicted by the Indians upon all who fell into their clutches. The outrages upon women were too horrible to be described. The forays extended into the Saline valley.

The Indians had kept the treaty that had been

made at Medicine Lodge the previous year only until the moment the grass was green enough to feed their ponies and bring back the buffaloes. The Indian was able to live and flourish solely upon buffalo meat, and so long as he had buffalo meat he would eat no other, not even venison, antelope or wild turkey.

Cox loaded his six hundred mules and his drivers aboard train and we started over the Kansas Pacific for Fort Hays. This railroad now extended as far west as Denver. We reached Fort Hays October 15, 1868. The fall was cold and disagreeable with lots of rain. To add to our discomfort, really our misery, we found that all the mules, big fellows from Missouri and Kentucky, were as wild as wolves, not one of them having been broken. Worst of all there was no time to break them. The Government wanted supplies rushed forward with all possible haste to what was known as Camp of Supply, afterwards Camp Supply, a military garrison, at the junction of Beaver and Wolf creeks in what is now Woodward County, Oklahoma.

The "wild west" performances of recent years are tame affairs compared with the handling of those mules. It was with a feeling of desperation that each man crawled out of his warm bed in the half light of early morning, ate his breakfast and then went out into the raw, drizzly cold to harness his mules. Kicking, squealing and bucking, they wore out a man's patience, and he was tempted to use his six-shooter on the devilish animals. To get them harnessed and hitched and the wagons strung out was a Napoleonic job. Once on the road, however, there was little to do beyond holding the mules in line, as the wagons were too heavily loaded for the mules to run away. When everything was moving, there were one hundred wagons and six hundred mules going down the trail. Our discomfort was increased by the fact that much of the time the ground was covered with snow. Our supplies were to equip Custer's command, which later was to fight the battle of the Washita and wipe out Black Kettle and his band. Next, Sheridan whipped the hostiles so badly that they never fully recovered their courage. The Indians were subdued mostly by a winter campaign, something they had never experienced. They were caught between the guns of the soldiers and the necessity of having food, shelter and warmth for their families and feed for their ponies. Defeat was inevitable under such dire circumstances.

The first day out we got to Smoky Hill River and camped for the night. We then pulled to Walnut Creek, and the third day brought us to Pawnee Fork. Between this place and what is now the town of Bucklin, Kas., we had a stampede that for real excitement beat anything I had ever seen. The mules ran in every possible direction, overturning wagons, and outfit colliding with outfit until it looked as if there would never be a pound of freight delivered at Supply. Many of the wagons were so badly demolished that they had to be abandoned and left behind. Their loads were piled on other wagons and carried forward.

Our route carried us past Saw Log Creek, Fort Dodge—there was no Dodge City at that time— Mulberry Creek, and thence to Bluff Creek. Here we sighted buffalo, the first we had seen on the trip. As we advanced further from the border of civilization buffalo grew more plentiful, so plentiful that between Bluff Creek and the Cimarron a big herd of stampeding buffalo bore squarely down upon our train. Things looked squally, as there was danger, not only of being run over by the buffaloes but of our mules running away, a disaster that would have been costly. A troop of cavalry was deployed to drive back or turn the oncoming herd. Every man in the outfit got out his gun, and we were able to give the buffaloes a reception that brought many of them to the ground, saved the mule train, and filled our pots and skillets with fine meat.

We reached Camp Supply at the end of a twelve days' journey. The supplies were unloaded on the ground and covered with tarpaulins. The site had been chosen by General Sully, upon the recommendation of an old scout, "Uncle John" Smith, who had been on the frontier about thirty years, and is said to have been the first white man that ever visited the country bordering the two Canadians. We did not see a single Indian during the trip to Supply.

Returning to Fort Hays, we made a second trip

down without mishap. But trouble was in store for us on our way back. The unloaded wagons were comparatively light, and the mules could easily pull them. We were driving two wagons abreast. Nobody ever knew what scared one of the rear teams, but it certainly got scared, and that particular outfit was soon going in the direction of Missouri and Kentucky at the rate of about thirty miles an hour. The rattling and banging and jolting of the wagon, and the shouting and swearing of the driver caused a tumult that spread panic among other teams and the stampede quickly reached the lead teams. So here we went, in every possible direction. It was impossible to hold the mules. Wagons were overturned, broken and scattered over the prairie for miles, and some of the mules were so badly crippled that they had to be shot. Some tore themselves loose from their harness and ran so far away that they were never found. The spectacle of those six hundred mules running away with their one hundred wagons was the most remarkable I ever witnessed.

One outfit, including both the wagon and the six mules, disappeared completely, I found them in 1871 when I was hunting buffalo on that range. The wagon and the carcasses of the mules were in a draw, or small canyon, about twelve miles from where the stampede began. In their headlong course, the mules could not stop when they came to the brink of the draw, so in they went, with the wagon piling on top of them. They were still hitched to the wagon, but badly tangled in the harness. In the wagon was an Army needle-gun, which showed that I was the first person to reach the spot.

After this experience, the mules were harder than ever to control, and would "run at the drop of the hat" or the flip of a prairie dog's tail.

Fort Hays at this time was the supply point for all the Government forts to the south, and remained as such until the Santa Fe railroad came through in the fall of 1872. I remained at Fort Hays until the fall of 1869, and this was my last work for the Government until 1874, when I was employed as a scout and guide under General Miles. During the five years I had been making my own way in the world, I had worked for the Government most of the time.

I was now eighteen years old, in perfect health, strong and muscular, with keen eyesight, a natural aptitude for outdoor life, was an excellent shot, and had a burning desire to experience every phase of adventure to be found on the Plains. I had worked all the summer of 1869 with George Smith and Tom Campbell, and liked them so well that we had planned fitting up an outfit to hunt and trap that winter. So along in November the three of us bought a good team and wagon, traps and provisions, and guns and ammunition and started north along the Saline River. Campbell was an old trapper and knew how to take beaver, which were fairly plentiful along the streams.

WOOD HAULER FOUND SCALPED NEAR FORT DODGE

My happiness now seemed complete, and I enjoyed to the fullest every moment of my life. Storm nor darkness nor hunger nor toil cooled my ardor in the slightest degree. We caught not only beaver, but several otter. Wolves abounded everywhere, and we trapped a large number. Their pelts were worth from $2.50 to $3 each. In this way we put in the winter, and made good money. We had a warm, comfortable dugout, with plenty of wood and water. I had no wish to return to a city. At intervals we would take a load of game to Hays City, where there was a ready market. Once we took in a load of elk, and got twenty dollars apiece for the carcasses.

The hunting of buffalo for their hides began in the spring of 1870. That was also the beginning of the destruction of the buffalo. As I remember, the hunting was started by a firm of eastern hidebuyers whose agents came to Hays City and other towns near the buffalo range and offered prices that made hide-hunting a profitable occupation.

We were in the very heart of the best buffalo country between the Dominion of Canada and the Rio Grande, and quickly abandoned trapping for buffalo hunting. The first offers were $1 each for cowhides and $2 each for bull hides, which enabled us to make money rapidly. As the slaughter increased and the buffalo grew scarcer, prices were advanced, until $4 was being paid for bull hides by the fall of 1872.

During the winter of 1870 we ranged all over

western Kansas, but principally along the Republican River and its tributaries. Generally, there were three or four men in an outfit, each having contributed his share for necessary expenses. They went where the range was best and buffalo most plentiful. A dugout was built and occupied as permanent headquarters camp, the hunters ranging for miles through the surrounding country. The only kind of dugout worth having was one with a big, open fire-place, near the edge of a stream of good water, with plenty of wood along its banks. We often occupied the same dugout for a month or more. Then, as the buffalo grew less plentiful, we shifted our camp and built a new dugout, which was easily and quickly done.

From where the buffalo were killed on the range, we hauled the hides to camp, where we dried them, then hauled them to market. Though I was not quite eighteen years of age, there were very few men who could excel me in marksmanship, which possibly was a natural gift supplemented by more or less constant practice.

I always did my own killing, and generally had two experienced men to do the skinning. A capable man could skin fifty buffalo a day, and usually was paid $50 a month. I have paid as much as twenty-cents a hide to a good skinner. We often killed the buffalo the day before they were to be skinned.

During the fall, Smith and Campbell grew tired of the business and wanted to quit. I bought the outfit, and straightway hired two men to work for me, and started out killing buffalo more energetically than ever. One of my skinners was a Mexican and the other a man named Perkins.

Up to this time I had hunted north of the Kansas Pacific railroad, and as far west as Fort Wallace. As the fall advanced, I began ranging further south, as the buffalo were becoming somewhat scarce. I was moving toward a country of future trouble—trouble with Indians—and to a region where in time I should meet with more adventure than I had ever dreamed of.

We moved south of Hays City about ten miles and came to a boiling spring that flowed from an opening in solid rock. Here we decided to make our permanent camp for the winter, so we built a picket house and a big dugout, expecting to dry a lot of buffalo meat for market, but finally abandoned this scheme. Our camp was on a main-traveled road leading to Hays City. Freighters and hunters urged me to establish a road ranch or store, where such supplies as were used in that country could be purchased in reasonable quantities. Having some spare money, I stocked up with tobacco, whisky and a general line of groceries, and employed a man named Billy Reynolds to run the place for me, while I devoted my time to killing buffaloes. Many a jolly company gathered at the road ranch at the boiling spring. The sale of whisky was a common practice in those days, as whisky was freely used by frontiersmen, and its sale

was expected as a matter of course. Other conditions were too hard and too pressing for the question of the morals of the traffic to be raised as it
was in later years, when the country became more
thickly settled, and an entirely new order of things
was established.

I was well acquainted with Reynolds and liked
him, having formed his acquaintance on the Custer
expedition to Camp Supply in 1868 when he was
a mule-driver. He was a friendly, whole-souled
kind of fellow, and knew just how to treat men to
get their trade. I made good money out of this
venture until 1871, when the income abruptly and
permanently ceased—during my absence Reynolds
sold the whole outfit and skipped the country,
without even telling me good-bye. I had been absent two weeks when I returned one day to find
only the empty building. I never again heard of
Billy Reynolds. I doubt that his robbing me was
ever to his final advantage. Money obtained in
that way never brought good luck, even in the
Plains country, where men were judged by rougher
standards than prevailed farther east.

I formed another partnership with a man named
Finn, who was square and honest, and sold him an
interest in the business. I had known him a number of years. He added another good team to the
outfit. He had been a Government teamster and
had served in the Civil War. He was a good story-
teller, and when the day's work was done, and we
were comfortably seated around the fire, nothing

pleased me more than to get Finn started telling stories. He was a native of Ireland, and the Irish brogue and humor gave a fine spice to his tales.

Finn and I hunted together about a year. During this time I had for a skinner another Irishman, a man named Mike McCabe. Mike had red hair, and a fiery temper. But he was a fine fellow, and I thought a great deal of him. He was one of the best workers I ever saw. Mike would fight at the drop of the hat, and again would sulk for weeks at a time over a fancied wrong. The men nicknamed him "Cranky" or "Fighting" McCabe. When he was in good humor a livelier fellow could not be found, but the moment he got a grouch he clouded up like a Panhandle thunderstorm.

The only thing in the world McCabe was afraid of was an Indian, of which I shall write later. Though small in size, McCabe would fight a man twice his size, and always give a good account of himself. His consuming passion was gambling, and when he struck town he invariably lost every-thing he had at the card table. He worked for me, off and on, for three years, and was with me at the fight at Adobe Walls.

During the time McCabe was with my outfit the two of us got along amicably, save when he would imagine that the world was against him, whereupon in a great huff he would quit, draw all his pay, and strike out for the nearest town—and its first gambling house within his reach. There he would remain until his last dollar was gone. Some fine morning McCabe would show up with beaming face and good-natured blarney, take his old job, and work even better than before.

Once he had been sulking for almost a week and had not spoken to a man in camp. When we started hunting, we decided to pull out and leave him at the ranch alone, which we did. After making our kill of buffaloes, we started back. When we got in sight of the ranch we were astonished at seeing McCabe dancing on a dry buffalo robe stretched on the ground. He was giving all the fancy steps and dancing as if a full orchestra were playing. Upon seeing us, he stopped dancing, and seemed chagrined. He had been entertaining himself. His conduct was rather laughable.

I rarely ever made a full settlement with Mc-Cabe, as he preferred to draw his pay in installments. I paid him fifty dollars a month. Sometimes he would have several hundred dollars ahead, and again he would be considerably overdrawn. Finally, he decided he would quit for good. Getting down to the job of settlement, I carefully figured each item and found that just two dollars were due him, whereupon he said, with a twinkle in his eye, "It beats the devil that a man should work three long years and get just two dollars." He went away in good humor, and we were always warm friends.

Finn and I were together until the next fall. He then took a notion to go back east and visit his folks, whom he had not seen since the Civil War. He was a frugal man, and did not smoke, chew tobacco, or drink whisky. His share of the year's work amounted to $5,000, which gave him a pretty good stake. He went to Rochester, New York, invested his money and was soon doing a profitable business. Several years afterwards he wrote to me saying that he longed to come back to the Plains country and its free life, but he never came.

Before Finn went away we had taken into partnership a man named Jack Callahan, who had been a Government wagonmaster at Fort Hays. Jack never saw the dark side of things, and was a delightful companion. During the winter of 1871 Jack and I were hunting on the headwaters of Pawnee Fork, drifting back and forth from there to Smoky Hill and Walnut Creek and their tributaries. Our permanent camp was on Hackberry Creek, a branch of Pawnee Fork. Along in November we had one of the worst blizzards I ever saw. It was this terrible storm that caught a wagon train loaded with cordwood for Hays City. This was Snuffer's bull train. All the cattle froze to death. The men were in a frightful condition when found. The outfit had been to Camp Supply with freight, and on the return trip had loaded up with cordwood on Walnut Creek.

The storm struck them just as they went into camp for the night, after the stock had been turned loose to gaze. When the storm broke, every man turned out to help hold the stock, and many of them were soon lost in the blinding swirl. One man, the cook, managed to find his way back to camp; he was found dead in his wagon, frozen stiff. Where he had tried to make a fire in the bottom of the wagon could be plainly seen. He had burned the endgate in his vain efforts. The wind blew with such terriffic force that the fire was blown away in all directions. Though surrounded with enormous quantities of wood, all within easy reach, the poor fellow perished for want of fire.

There was hardly a man in this ill-fated outfit who did not suffer the loss of a hand, a foot, or a limb. The men were camped in Five Mile Hollow, five miles from Hays City, and when news of the affair reached town next day, all the citizens turned out to search for the missing men, gathering them up and taking them to the hospital at Hays City. Some of the bewildered men wandered to my road-ranch, where Billy Reynolds was in charge, and there found shelter and protection from the storm.

A few days after the storm had abated I decided to make a trip to Hays City, and bring back supplies for the outfit, so I hooked four mules to a wagon and hitched my saddle horse to the side. I rarely ever went out on the road without my saddle horse. The mules seemed to be more contented when accompanied by a horse, and in case of trouble I stood a better show of getting away on horseback.

Our camp was on Hackberry, and I went prepared to stay all night with Reynolds at the road-ranch, the first night out. When I got there I found the place deserted. I could not imagine why Reynolds was not there and did not learn the reason until I reached Hays, driving there that night. I saw Snuffer's wagons corralled at Five Mile Hollow when I passed that place, but heard nothing of what had happened until I got to Hays. Here I learned the no less surprising news that Reynolds had sold everything at the road-ranch and had skipped the country.

The day after I reached town the express agent came into the hotel office where I was stopping and asked if a man could be found who would take a load of express to Fort Dodge or Camp Supply, saying that there was a lot of express for both places. As I had a good team, and there was no great need of my hurrying back to headquarters, I told him that I would go. I also wanted to look that country over for buffalo.

I loaded and started for Fort Dodge with fifteen hundred pounds of express, making Walnut Creek the first night and staying at a road-ranch run by Johnny Quinn, afterward killed at that place. The weather was bitter cold when I started next morning, and by 10 o'clock it was spitting snow and getting colder every minute. I walked part of the time to keep warm. My load was bulky rather than heavy. I felt the cold driving into my very bones, and realized my danger. I was determined that I would not permit myself to sink into drowsiness, as this meant death. Reaching a long divide, I dropped down the slope with my mules in a gallop, and luckily was soon in sight of a road-ranch kept by John O'Loughlin. I was scarcely able to speak when I drove up and found half a dozen men coming to meet me, all eager to hear the news from town, whatever it might be. In answer to their questions I merely shook my head. My jaws were set like a vice. I could not speak a word. They saw instantly my condition. Running into the dugout they began piling wood into the fire-place, and the room was soon as hot as an oven. I thawed gradually, burning like a live coal one moment and shivering the next as if I had a fit of ague. This was my first experience with killing cold. In later days, after I became a Government scout, I had many similar experiences. I once made a ride with dispatches, and became so stiff with cold by the time I had reached the end of my journey that I could not dismount from my horse —I simply let go and fell off.

In the Pawnee Fork and Saw Log country I had seen lots of buffalo, a sight which always held me with extreme fascination. When I got to Fort Dodge the third night out I heard that the buffalo had drifted in by thousands during the blizzard, and that the garrisons had to fire a piece of artillery to keep them from breaking down the buildings and corrals.

Next day I mounted my horse and struck off up the Arkansas to look over the country, traveling up the valley for about thirty-five miles. There had certainly been an enormous number of buffalo in the country. I could see where the grass had been flattened and the willow thickets cropped close by the tired and hungry animals. In every direction could be seen the spots where the buffaloes had bedded down for the night. But now there was not a buffalo in sight.

Lured on by the hope of catching sight of the vast multitude that had passed that way, I kept on up the valley, but without success. Then I determined to proceed to the Plains, which I did. Riding to a high point I turned my eyes across the Plains. I held my breath in my astonishment at the wonderful sight. As far as I could see there was a solid mass of buffalo, quietly grazing on the curly mesquite, now brown with winter. At no other time in my life did I ever see such a vast number of buffalo. For miles in every direction the country was alive with them.

At this point I want to say that in all my experience in the buffalo country I never saw one die of old age and exhaustion, and can remember seeing only one "on the lift"—that is, in a situation where he could go no further. This one, an old bull, had got fast in a bog on the Canadian, and was unable to get out. Riding up to him. I threw my lariat over his head, after I had given my lariat a hitch over the born of my saddle, and pulled the old fellow to firm ground. I left him grazing contentedly on the bank. The buffalo was a hardy animal, and though they often got very thin during a hard winter, yet they never became so thin and starved as to go off their feet like cattle.

I returned to Fort Dodge fully satisfied with my day's ride, and next day started on my return trip to Fort Hays. By the time I reached Fort Hays, a considerable number of hunters had been driven in by the storm. I told them of the black ocean of buffalo I had seen northwest of Fort Dodge, which was good news to them, and set every man to overhauling his outfit.

I was impatient to reach my camp, so I loaded up with supplies and pulled out. I found the boys in good shape and glad to see me. Next day we made a scout out west of Hackberry, and found thousands of buffalo. It was plain that the big herd had drifted a long way during the blizzard, and had been as far south as the Arkansas. When the weather moderated they worked back to their old range.

Along in May, 1872, we moved our camp from Hackberry to a point north of the Kansas Pacific railroad.

While in camp on Hackberry I met with an experience which rarely ever happened to me—I got completely lost, so badly that I had no idea of direction. Perkins and I had been out all day killing and skinning buffalo. We had worked late, and it had grown cloudy and dark before we started for camp. Both were afoot. In moving from each fallen buffalo to another we had wandered farther than we suspected. Each thought camp was in a different direction. So positive was Perkins that he was right that I followed him for a time.

I was relying mostly upon the direction of the buffalo trails and when I found that we were crossing them instead of following them, I was convinced that we had lost our bearings. I called Perkins' attention to the trails. He insisted that he was going in the right direction. Perkins was a windy story-teller, and was relating a war tale. I disliked to interrupt him. Finally, however, I said that unless the wind had changed we were certainly going in the wrong direction.

"Oh, the wind has changed," he replied. "I knew it would this morning."

About this time we reached the head of a draw, cn which we thought our camp was situated. At that moment the clouds drifted from the face of the moon, and we saw a bunch of buffalo that had bedded down for the night. This convinced me that Perkins was "going it wild," as I was sure that buffalo would not stay that close to our camp.

Rovers that we were, with sails turned for every wind, we decided to kill some of tbe buffaloes, as they would be conveniently at hand, for skinning next morning, and we shot five or six.

Pursuing our way down the draw, I was soon positive that we were lost. Perkins put up a lively argument to prove that he was not mistaken. When we reached another bunch of buffalo that had bedded. Perkins threw up the sponge. Four bulls were lying together. We blazed into them, made a warm bed of two hides, with the hair turned inside, and made a dry camp for the night. We slept as warm as if we had been in a feather bed, though the night was cold.

In after years I thought many times of that night on the Plains. Of how tired we were, of how the wind whistled past us, of how the cold seemed to come down out of the sky, heavy and chill, and of how icily the moon shone as she sailed westward. Save for the occasional howling of wolves and coyotes, the night was supernaturally silent. It was the stillness of the primeval solitude. It was the stuff that makes a man in a warm bed under a roof feel like getting up to saddle his horse and ride away to this Land of Nowhere. Once in the blood, it can never be lost. Home-sickness for the Plains and their free, open life stings like a hornet.

Perkins and I slept late next morning. The sun was shining in my face when I heard something scratching and clawing on the hide with which we were covered. There were lots of skunks in the country, and lately several men had been bitten by them. I thought of skunks, of which I stood in dread, as I would have preferred being bitten by a rattlesnake.

Bracing myself, I kicked the hide with all my might, to throw it as far as possible from both of us. Instead of a skunk, I was astonished to see a big eagle that had been trying to get his breakfast by picking the meat off the fresh hide. That eagle was so badly scared that I am sure he must have had an attack of heart failure. He flopped around before he could get up enough steam to take wing, and even then he hovered in the air as if uncertain which way to fly. I could have killed him with the butt of my gun. I had no wish to do this, however, and watched him recover his wits and soar away.

I do not believe that I exaggerate when I say that Perkins jumped five feet into the air when I kicked off the buffalo hide. He told me that he was sure Indians had nailed us, and that his scalp-lock twitched all day.

Coming out of the draw where we had made our bed, we ascended a high point and scanned the surrounding country, hoping to locate our camp. Nothing looked familiar to us. We struck out in the direction we thought camp ought to be. We walked until nearly night before we got back to camp.

By noon I was growing ravenously hungry. I suggested to Perkins that we kill a buffalo and broil some of the meat. We shot a 2-year-old heifer, and soon had a hump steak sizzling on the fire. No meal ever gave me greater satisfaction, though we had no salt or bread.

We were fagged and footsore when we reached camp. James Donnelly, the man we had left at camp, had given us up as dead, confident that we had been killed by Indians. He had packed the outfit, harnessed the mules, and was just at the point of pulling out for Hays City when we hailed him. We would have been left in bad shape had he gone. During the morning a band of twelve or fifteen Indians had passed in sight of camp, and as we had been missing two days and one night, Donnelly naturally concluded that the Indians had killed us. After he saw the Indians he made up his mind that the best thing for him to do was to leave as quickly as possible for the Fort.

During the summer of 1872 we hunted along the Saline and Solomon, frequently encountering small bands of Indians. Generally, they were going north or south, and though they were supposed to be friendly, we watched them closely. Occasionally, we heard of a hunter being killed, but this did not bother us, so long as we were not molested. Sometimes, Indians came into our camp. They were always hungry. We always fed them. They love sugar and coffee, and for either were willing to trade anything they had. The Kiowas were especially fond of sugar. The liking for sweet things is not peculiar to the white man.

CHAPTER V

WE started south to the Arkansas River in the fall of 1872, and when we got to where Dodge City now stands, we found the first buildings under construction. None of us dreamed of the reputation that was to come to that town through its gun men. There were only a few houses at Dodge. I remember that the Cox House, the first hotel, was open. Deciding to "put on airs," we went to the hotel for dinner. Our bill of fare was pork and beans, black coffee, bread and pepper sauce, especially pepper sauce, for which we paid seventy-five cents. We could have beat it, hands down, in our own camp. I can recall the names of a number of the first business establishments:

Wright & Company ("Bob" Wright), general supply store.

Zimmerman's hardware, gun and ammunition store.

McCart & Fringer, drug store. Fringer afterwards was judge of Ford County court.

Kelly & Beaty, saloon. Kelly was a jolly, good-natured man, and was always popular. He was always called "Dog" Kelly.

Murray & Waters, saloon.

Beeson & Harris, saloon.

Hoover's saloon.

The buildings were mostly box affairs, and built in the quickest possible way. But a palace does not make happiness, and I am sure that in the rough, frontier towns of those days there was lots of contentment and good cheer in the rudest shacks. The wind and the snow came in at the cracks in winter, and in summer the rain beat through and the red dust swirled along the floor, but we paid little attention to such things. Our skin was tough and we had many things to occupy our time. We were constantly in the open air, which hardened us until we suffered scarcely any annoyance from wind or weather, such as would have been looked upon as hardships not to be endured, by men living cooped up in cities, where there is rarely a chance to fill one's lungs with fresh air and where heaviest clothing cannot compensate for lack of physical exercise. It is possible by exposure for men to toughen their skin and their bodies, just as they can toughen their hands. The Indian is a good example of this fact.

At this time Dodge City was the terminus of the Santa Fe railroad. The railroad company was still grading, as far west as Granada, Colo., where building stopped for about a year. Dodge City sprang up like a mushroom. Buildings went up day and night, and in a month's time the first dozen houses had been increased to a small town.

Like moths drawn by the flame of a lamp, a picturesque lot of men gathered at Dodge. Practically all of them were looking for adventure and excitement, rather than for opportunities to become preachers, lawyers or merchants. They came from the border towns that dotted like beads that western fringe of civilization. Dodge City belonged mostly to the under-world in those days, and its ways were the ways of men and women who stayed up all night and slept all day. Buffalo-hunters, railroad graders, gamblers, dance hall actors and dancers and that nondescript class that lived without doing any kind of work predominated. But there were good men and women in Dodge, and as in most genuine American communities, they finally won out, despite its revelries and dissipations. The professional gun man that gave Dodge most of its reputation, especially in eastern states, did not ply his business as a business until later years.

Money was plentiful in those days. Anybody could get money, and there was no excuse for being "broke." Business thrived, and some of the stores could supply a man with practically anything he needed. The men of Dodge City spent their money as quickly as they made it, so lots of money was constantly in circulation. Whisky-drinking was a pastime or diversion in which few men did not indulge. It was true, however, that some of Dodge City's most famous characters never drank a drop of intoxicating liquors. They did not dare do it. They belonged to the class known as "killers." To get drunk or to drink enough whisky to make the nerves unsteady meant death for such men, as the enemy was always lying in wait for them.

I knew of one instance where a man lost all he had gambling at Dodge City. He was known as Dirty Faced Jones. I never heard any other name for him; it was said he never washed his face. Jones was very close and stingy and had never been known to gamble. He had saved up about $2,000 and had a lot of buffalo hides on hand ready to sell when a woman persuaded him to take a chance at the roulette table. At first he won but luck turned against him and he lost all the money he had in one night. He was so disgusted that he sold everything he had and left the country.

I cannot boast of having been an altogether perfect man in my conduct in those wild, free days, but there were two popular forms of amusement in which I did not indulge—dancing and gambling. I never bet a nickel on cards nor gambled in any form in my life, though I saw all these things going on every night when I was in a border town, especially at Dodge. Why I did not, rather than the mere fact that I did not, has always been to me a matter of interest and speculation. My only answer would be that this sort of thing did not appeal to me, and this was sufficient beyond any moral reason for my conduct.

As a class, the early population of Dodge was free-hearted and would divide the last dollar with a friend or a stranger in distress. The people stood by each other in all emergencies. Nobody thought of locking his door at night.

When the Santa Fe's construction was stopped at Granada, hundreds of men were thrown out of employment, and found it necessary to make some kind of shift for work, or leave the country. Right here is where the rapid extermination of the buffalo began. All of these men who could rustle a team and a wagon and get hold of an outfit went out on the Plains to kill buffalo. During the fall and winter of 1872 and 1873 there were more hunters in the country than ever before or afterwards. Thus came the high tide of buffalo-hunting. More were killed that season than in all subsequent seasons combined. I feel safe in saying that 75,000 buffalo were killed within sixty or seventy-five miles of Dodge City during that time. The noise of the guns of the hunters could be heard on all sides, rumbling and booming hour after hour, as if a heavy battle were being fought. There was a line of camps all the way from Dodge City to Granada.

Throughout the time since 1871 Jack Callahan and I had worked together. Perkins and Donnelly were still with us. "Cranky" McCabe, his good humor having revived, came back to work for me. A single night at the card table in Dodge City generally wound up McCabe's ball of yarn, and at once he was ready to return to the buffalo range without complaint. Apparently, there was something he had to get out of his system, and after he had been purged he was ready to resume his old ways. There was not a lazy bone in his body, and I never had a better hand. I was very much attached to Jack Callahan. He was always in good humor, which is a fine quality for a man to have in a hunting camp. A bad temper can spoil the pleasure of an entire camp. Some mornings we would sleep late. When the sun got in his eyes, Jack would jump up, exclaiming "By George, this will never do! It will never buy my girl a dress nor pay for the one she has."

After we had been at Dodge City a few days, taking in the sights, we grew tired of loafing, and decided to strike out and go to new hunting grounds. So we went up the Arkansas River, along the north side, to what was known as Nine Mile Ridge, where we crossed to the south side of the river.

The increasing numbers and destructiveness of the buffalo-hunters had been making the Plains Indians more and more hostile. The danger to hunters was increasing day by day. All that region south of the Arkansas was forbidden ground, the Indians insisting that the white men should obey the terms of the Medicine Lodge treaty. If the killing of the buffalo should continue unabated, the Indians would soon be facing starvation; at least, their old freedom would be at an end, as they could no longer roam the country at will, confident of finding meat in abundance wherever they might go.

The Arkansas was called the "dead line," south of which no hunter should go. The river was patrolled at intervals by Government troops, as a feeble indication that the Medicine Lodge treaty had not been forgotten, but their vigilance was so lax that there was no difficulty in crossing back and forth without detection. The danger of attack by Indians was a far more potent obstacle to the buffalo-hunter, but as buffalo grew fewer in number and the price of hides advanced, even this did not deter hardy hunters from undertaking forays into the forbidden country. The troops were supposed to prevent the passing of the Indians to the north side of the river. This patrol also failed to work.

We gazed longingly across the sandy wastes that marked the course of the Arkansas. The oftener we looked the more eager we became to tempt fate. Even the sky looked more inviting in that direction, and often after a flurry of cold weather the wind from the south was mild, balmy and inviting. As a matter of fact, the possible danger of encountering hostile Indians added spice to the temptation.

So we crossed over. Finding a pleasant stretch of bottom land, where the grass grew tall and thick, we cut and stacked a lot of prairie hay for our teams and saddle horses. The grass waved above our horses' backs as we rode along. Later, we found Indians too numerous in this vicinity for us to devote much time to hunting and we abandoned this camp.

Before we made the change, however, Callahan and I, both well mounted, and followed by one man in a light wagon, started, southward on a scouting trip, intending to be gone several days. We wanted to feel out the country and locate the buffalo herds.

When we reached Crooked Creek, we ran smack into a bunch of Indians, and had a skirmish with them. The Indians could not speak English. This did not prevent our understanding them. Their old chief motioned to us to go northward. That was a long time ago, yet I remember clearly the appearance of this old warrior. Conspicuously fastened under the skin of his left cheek he wore a long, brilliant feather. All the warriors were painted red and yellow. We believed, however, that we were able to take care of ourselves, and continued on our way. Further down the creek, we struck another band of hostiles. This was rather too much of the same thing, and we decided that if we valued our scalps we had better pull out.

We turned round and headed for camp, missing it about three miles in the darkness, and going into camp for the night in the enemy's country. Next morning we got back in safety, and called all hands round to discuss the situation. Plainly, to stay south of the Arkansas meant putting in more time fighting Indians than in hunting buffalo.

But buffalo had begun coming in by thousands, so we agreed to remain two or three days and make as big a kill as possible. Hunting was good, and a week had slipped by. The hides were green, which forced us to linger until they were dry. Not only were hides more easily handled when dry, but they made lighter loads.

About the ninth day, we found ourselves running short of meat. A bunch of buffalo were grazing about two miles distant. Mounting my horse, I told the boys that I would ride out and kill two good ones for meat. I was so well acquainted with the ways of buffalo that I could judge quickly by their actions whether they would run or stand when approached. I saw that these were getting ready to run.

This fact was a plausible hint that Indians were moving through the country. My own experience and the testimony of other hunters convinced me that nothing causes greater alarm among buffalo than the odor of Indians, an odor likewise easily distinguished by a white man's nostrils. When Indian hunting parties went on the buffalo grounds to get their winter's supply of meat, the herds were soon in great commotion, making it difficult for the white hunter to do his killing at a "stand." Strange as it may seem, if there were no Indians moving among the buffaloes, the latter would pay scarcely any attention to white hunters, even though the big buffalo guns were booming from sunrise to sunset.

Upon nearing the buffalo as closely as I thought expedient, I dismounted and began crawling. Picking out a young bull, I turned loose with my big

"50" gun. The herd stampeded at the first crack, and raised such a dust that I could distinguish nothing. I fired as rapidly as I could pull the trigger at the indistinguishable mass, and was lucky enough to bring down six or seven before the herd was out of range.

This fusilade from my gun set things moving in camp, where the boys jumped to the conclusion that I had been attacked by Indians. To add to the excitement a herd of about fifty antelope appeared on a hill perhaps half a mile from camp. The swiftly running animals would traverse a wide circle and dash again to the top of the hill, where they would stand rigidly attentive gazing in my direction. The excited imagination of the boys in camp soon transformed these harmless creatures into mounted Indians. They had not the slightest doubt of my having been killed and scalped, my body left weltering in its own blood, and speared and arrowed until it resembled a sieve.

When I rode into camp a few minutes later, I found everything ready for flight and battle. All the fighting guns were conveniently at hand, and all the camp equipment was loaded on the wagon. The boys were just at the point of pulling out, but had lingered a moment to debate whether they should try to recover my dead body or whoop her up for Dodge City.

Jack Callahan was declaring that it would be wrong to go away without being sure that I was dead. While this discussion was under way each man was as busy as a coon in a hen roost. McCabe had been set at work priming a lot of shells, which were already loaded. In his excitement he held the primers in his left hand, asking all the while, "Where in thunder are those primers? I can't find a single one, yet I saw a lot of them only a moment ago. Unless we get these shells primed, we'll be in bad shape!"

McCabe was so nervous that the primers rattled in his shaking hand, without his seeing them. McCabe lived in mortal terror of Indians, though as brave as a lion under all other emergencies, a peculiarity I have seen in other men on the Plains. The scent or odor of the Indian affected some men as it did certain animals other than the buffalo. All kinds of game seemed to know when an Indian was around. A horse could be safely depended upon to give warning of the near approach of an Indian. I have had my horse run to and fro on his picket rope, manifesting the greatest alarm, apparently without cause, as I could see nothing. I never failed, however, to find later that an Indian had been close by.

The boys gazed at me in utmost astonishment as I rode into camp, safe and sound. They could not believe that I had really returned, and began asking me a thousand questions. We laughed over what had happened, each teasing the other about having been "scared out of a year's growth." All save McCabe took the joking in good nature. When the boys began poking fun at him about

losing the primers, McCabe slashed on his war
paint and squared off to fight. He shouted that
he would fight with bare fists, with a butcher knife
or with a gun whoever repeated the story. He
would have done as he threatened, but all of us
liked him and only laughed at him the more.

We loaded up with hides next day and pulled
out for Dodge City, where we were lucky enough
to strike a good market. We had to make three
trips to get all the hides, for which we received
from $2.50 to $4 apiece, the highest price we ever received. The full amount was $1,975, but the buyer
wrote us a check for the even sum of $2,000, a little
matter like $25 being of no moment in those days
at Dodge City.

The weather was now growing much colder,
warning us that we should prepare for snow, sleet
and howling blizzards. Each man bought himself
a supply of warm winter clothing, and with lots of
supplies and ammunition, we again went in search
of the shaggy buffalo. We went up the Arkansas
as far west as the next railroad station, where we
hunted a few days, finding buffaloes so scarce that
we moved over on the head of South Pawnee.

I had been over this country the previous year,
and knew where there was a splendid spring of
water, which I discovered in an unusual manner.
On a hot, sultry August day I had left my horse
down in the valley, and wandered off on foot after
a bunch of buffaloes, going much further than I
suspected at the time. Growing very thirsty, I

began casting about for signs of water. Crossing the head of a small "draw," I saw a patch of green about a quarter of a mile distant. I hastened toward the spot, and there, to my astonishment, found a spring of clear, sweet water that boiled from a crevice in the rock. In after years I thought many times of the delightful sensation of lying beside that spring and drinking until I could drink no more. While resting, I carved in full my name, "William Dixon," in the soft sandstone rock at the head of the spring. Many years later, when I was living at Plemons, the county seat of Hutchinson County, Texas, I met a land agent who told me that he had seen my name on a rock at the head of a spring in western Kansas. He had no idea that he was talking to the man who carved the name. This man said that the country was thickly settled by prosperous farmers, which seemed incredible when I recalled the days when its principal inhabitants were buffaloes, mustangs, Indians and buffalo hunters.

We shifted camp as soon as the buffalo began thinning in numbers. Reaching North Pawnee, we went up as far as Walnut Creek, changing our camp as the buffaloes shifted, and finally going back south to Silver Lake, ten miles north of the Arkansas River. This lake was out on the open Plains.

Here we were struck by another blizzard. There were two outfits camped at Silver Lake. The "norther" struck us with terrific fury, and caught us short of fuel, other than buffalo "'chips." I wish here to say something in honor of the buffalo chip. In later years, as the fortunes of the settlers in western Kansas improved and their social aspirations grew stronger, there were those who looked askance upon the humble buffalo chip, though they had seen the time when they were devoutly grateful for the genial warmth that spread from its glowing fire. It was the friend and benefactor of countless hunters and settlers in hours of need and extremity. The buffalo chip was simply the dry dung of the buffalo, purely vegetable, and made an excellent fire, over which coffee could be boiled and meat fried to a turn. When dry the buffalo chip caught the flame easily, and soon burned to a dull red. Many a dark night have I looked with gladness at the distant buffalo chip fire, knowing that around it I would find hospitable companions and lots of warmth.

There was a big scramble to make snug when the norther hit us. As soon as it broke, we tied buffalo hides to the wagons to form a shelter for our horses, but the wind was so strong that it tore down the hides and carried them rattling and bounding across the Plains. Worst of all, the gale blew all the fire out of our camp stoves. We were forced to go to bed to keep from freezing to death, and we remained wrapped in our blankets under our buffalo robes until next day.

I am sure that in these later years we do not have the sudden blizzards, such as swept howling from the north in those early days, which is fortunate, as they would cause untold suffering to people and livestock.

The weather had moderated by next day, and we went in search of our stock, which we found at John O'Loughlin's road-ranch, twelve miles south of Silver Lake. As there was snow on the ground and it was difficult to find fuel, even buffalo chips, we decided to stay at O'Loughlin's place until the weather settled. Other hunters were in the same plight as ourselves, and they too came drifting in to O'Loughlin's. We were a jolly crowd. What sport we had, telling stories of our hunts, drinking whisky, playing cards and shooting at targets. I was especially fond of the latter.

In such a gathering there were always mischievous fellows forever scheming to play jokes and pranks upon their companions. While at O'Loughlin's a sham duel, one of the funniest things I ever saw, was pulled off.

Among the hunters was a young fellow who was continually stirring up trouble by quarreling. At O'Loughlin's he began imposing upon a quiet, peaceful man who never bothered anybody. The boys persuaded him to challenge the bully to fight a duel, telling him they would load the bully's gun with blank cartridges. The arrangements were soon made. The bully was willing to fight—at least he seemed to be. He was the only man in camp that did not know that the affair was a "frame up." The seconds were chosen, and the time and place of the meeting fixed. The weapons were to be six-shooters, at fifteen steps.

The buffalo hunters lined up to see the fight. The quiet fellow was to shoot over the bully's head, but close enough for him to hear the whistle of the bullet. At the command of "fire" both pistols cracked, but nobody was hit. The bully winced a bit at the sound of the bullet as it passed over his head. He soon went locoed, and became so badly frightened that he could hardly stand. His knees knocked together, and he trembled like a wet dog on a cold day. Before the second encounter could take place, the bully squawked, saying that he had enough. He was teased and rawhided until he left camp, and pulled out for pleasanter surroundings.

As soon as the weather grew warmer, the hunters went to their camps. We returned to Silver Lake, but not finding buffalo plentiful enough to make hunting profitable, we went over on what was known as White Woman's Fork, usually a dry stream, with water only in the rainy season. At this time the melting snow had formed pools. White Woman's Fork is between the Arkansas and the Smoky Hill.

Buffalo were so scarce that we followed White Woman's Fork to its head and thence went over to the brakes of the Smoky Hill, and from there we pulled to Sand Creek, in Colorado. While on Sand Creek we camped one night where the Chivington massacre of Cheyenne Indians took place in November, 1864. Chivington was in command of a force of Colorado troops, and took the Indians wholly by surprise. Among the Indians was Black Kettle's band of Cheyennes, afterward destroyed by General Custer on the Washita in Southwestern Oklahoma. Chivington gave orders to kill everything that looked like an Indian—women and children, old and young—and his command was obeyed with utmost cruelty. We could see bones still scattered over the battleground.

Our hunt for buffalo was proving to be a kind of wild goose chase. We had made a complete circle, without finding them in sufficient numbers to warrant our hunting in any one place. We went back down the Arkansas until we reached Lakin, Kansas, where we stayed eight or ten days gathering up the hides we had left at different places. We hauled them to Dodge City.

By this time the spring of 1873 was at hand. Callahan and I dissolved partnership, as Callahan wanted to go into the saloon business at Granada, Colorado. He lived there until General Miles started from Fort Dodge in 1874 on his campaign against the southwest Plains Indians. Callahan went along as wagon master.

I did not have enough of the buffalo game, however, and after going back to my old camp on Pawnee Fork, I crossed the Arkansas in May, 1873, and went up the river to what was known as Aubrey Crossing, on the old Santa Fe trail. Here we camped and explored the country, but failed to find many buffaloes, and began working south toward the Cimarron—toward the forbidden and dangerous land. We struck the Cimarron at what was known as Wagonbed Springs, southwest of Dodge. At that time the Cimarron River was called the dead line. Few hunters had gone south of the Arkansas. Many who had been hunting around Dodge in 1872 and 1873 had abandoned the hide business, because of the diminishing number of buffaloes, and for the better reason that they did not wish to follow the main herd into the Indian country.

Ranging between the Arkansas and the Cimarron in the summer of 1873, we worked west as far as Bear Creek, in Stanton County, Kansas. We prospered, as buffaloes were plentiful. Our hides were hauled to Granada, Colorado.

Along in the fall we went to Dodge and loaded up with supplies for an expedition even farther south. We struck Crooked Creek and finally the Cimarron, ten miles below Wagonbed Springs, where we planned to stay during the winter and built a dugout. Buffaloes were everywhere, but like the leaves of the winter forest—disappearing never to return.

While in camp at this place we saw a spectacular sight. A big war party of Cheyennes passed on their way to fight the Utes. The latter lived in Colorado. The Cheyennes were out for blood. Their horses were in fine shape, and each warrior was fully equipped with weapons. We learned that the Utes had long been in the habit of coming down to the buffalo country every fall to kill their winter's supply of meat. The Cheyennes, proud and arrogant, were opposed to this invasion of their hunting grounds by the mountain Indians and had decided to make an end of it if possible. Much has been written about the desperate warfare and the bloody battles between Indians and white men. I am rather of the opinion that war between Indian tribes was even worse. They fought to exterminate each other if possible.

This expedition of Cheyennes was divided into many small parties—three or four warriors traveling together. We had heard of their attacking other buffalo hunters, and running off their stock. We kept both eyes open, day and night. Frequently, these Indians would stop at our camp, to which we offered no objection if there were only a few in the party, but if fifteen or twenty came in sight, heading toward our camp, we signalled for them to pass around without stopping. We did not dare run the risk of letting a superior force of Indians get at close quarters under the guise of friendship, as soon every hunter's scalp would have been dangling on the Cheyenne bridles. Occasionally, the Cheyennes upon approaching would lay down their guns, and advance unarmed, to show that they did not intend to offer us injury. We always fed them well.

About fifteen warriors came into camp one day, and were soon greatly interested in a pair of field glasses that I used in looking over the country for landmarks, buffaloes and Indians. After letting our visitors look through them, I laid the glasses on a pile of bedding and thought no more about them. After the Indians had ridden away, I reached for the glasses to look over a bunch of Indians that had assembled on a hill a mile or so distant. The glasses had disappeared.

I was fighting mad, and determined to get my glasses or kill an Indian or two. Seizing my buffalo gun and mounting my best horse, I started in pursuit of the thieves. The rascals suspected my purpose, and long before I got within shooting range they scattered like quail and hid themselves. The country was rough and broken and I found it decidedly too dangerous to attempt to hunt them out.

In approaching our camp, it had been the practice of the Cheyennes to come with their horses running at headlong speed, possibly to "throw a scare" into the white men. We at once set our heads against this sort of thing, and soon convinced the Indians that we would fire into them if the practice were repeated.

All these Cheyennes were rigged out in full war style. Each had a led horse, his war horse, which was the Indian's pride, and which he loved above his other possessions. He gave his war horse the best of care, and kept him expressly for battle.

The detachments of this big Cheyenne war party were about three days passing our camp, and during that time we remained close at home. One

INDIAN CAMP OF BUFFALO HIDE TEPEES

of us constantly stood guard on a high point close by. There was smell of Indian in the air. Our horses were picketed during the day, and at night we tied them to the wagons. There were only four of us, and we could not afford to make the slightest mistake.

After the country was clear of Indians, we made a trip over on Sharpe's Creek, but found no buffalo —the passing of the Indians had scared the buffalo away. If the buffalo would not come to us, we would go to the buffalo; so we shifted camp from the Cimarron down to the Beaver, in "No Man's Land."

Making short drives each day, to spy out the country, we got as far west as the site of the present town of Guymon, Okla., where we camped several days to clean up several scattering bunches of buffalo, all bulls. These old bulls were easily killed, and their hides brought the best prices.

Here we met some of the same Cheyennes that had passed our camp on the Cimarron. They were on their way back home to Indian Territory. They recognized us. I had acquired some knowledge of the Cheyenne language, and questioned them about their trip to the Ute country. It was funny to hear them tell how they had "run the Utes clean over the mountains." They claimed they had killed stacks and stacks of Utes, going through the motions of how the Utes ran in getting away from the Cheyennes.

After making a kill of buffalo, the hides were

always left on the ground to dry, before hauling them to market. We had had left a big lot of hides and provisions at our Cimarron camp. The passing of the Indians on their way back home made us feel that it might be well to see what the situation was in our old camp. We expected to find all our hides gone and our provisions stolen; to our great surprise we found everything just as we had left it. The Plains Indians were highly suspicious, and it is possible that they feared the provisions might be poisoned.

The thinning out of the buffalo made hunting more difficult. Riding out early one morning, I managed to kill about thirty during the day's hunt, all of them cows. It was a strange fact that buffalo cows and bulls ranged together only during the breeding season; at other times they went in separate bunches.

Next morning we went out to do our skinning. Having run short of meat, I had drawn several of the carcasses, and was so busily engaged that I did not notice what was going on around me.

The day was warm, with the wind in the south. Then the wind died until there was perfect calm for about fifteen minutes. Suddenly, our attention was drawn to the unusual appearance of the sand-hills to the north of us, along the river. We could see a fog of dust and sand, which struck us in a shorter time than it takes to tell it. We were caught in the jaws of a norther, the terror of the plainsman. All animals seem to know instinctively when a norther is coming, and grow nervous and restless.

It is difficult to see or to breathe when a norther is at its height, and unless good shelter is near at hand there is danger of quickly freezing to death. We were wise enough to know that the best thing for us to do would be to get back to camp as quickly as possible. Tossing our meat into the wagon, we jumped in and headed for camp with our mules at a gallop. On my horse I rode beside the mules, urging them along with my quirt. Despite our instant flight and our speed, we were nearly frozen when we arrived at camp.

These winter storms usually exhausted themselves at the end of two or three days, but while they are raging it is impossible to leave camp with safety.

After we had thawed out, we decided to tackle the Beaver country again, and went up that stream to a place then known as Company M, where we struck off in a southwesterly direction and came to the Coldwater, which farther toward its source is known as Agua Frio, which means "cold water." It undoubtedly was named by the Mexicans who used to hunt in that region. The favorite weapon of these Mexicans was the lance, which necessarily brought them at close quarters with the buffalo and required swift horses.

The Coldwater takes its rise from a number of springs, locally known as Buffalo Springs, which form a series of remarkable pools of water. At this place afterward was built one of the headquarters of the old **XIT** Ranch outfit. The buildings stand today as they did in earlier years, but the phase of life that dwelt there has vanished forever. When the **XIT** established itself in the Texas Panhandle, the cowboy was typical, genuine and picturesque. He was the cock of the walk. He could "eat centipedes for breakfast and barbed wire for supper without injuring his digestion," and dance all night and ride all day without missing a step. His like will never be seen again. He had a tough hide and a tender heart, and an ear that was inclined to every hard luck story that passed his way.

Buffalo Springs stands in the open Plains south of the Beaver and just south of the line that divides the Texas Panhandle from Cimarron County, Oklahoma. Here is a considerable growth of timber, consisting of cottonwoods, elms and willows. The traveler will go many, many weary miles south before he again sees a clump of timber or finds living water.

The beginning of Agua Frio is a spring near a lone cottonwood tree about a mile west of the ranch house. The water rises in a fissure in the rock. Some rather fabulous stories have been told about its depth. Below it is a chain of deep pools of dark and steely clearness, chillingly cold even in hottest midsummer, with steep, precipitous banks, along which waves a dense and almost impenetrable growth of reeds and tall, wiry grass. Here abound bass in such size and numbers as to tempt the most expert angler.

Buffalo Springs is a veritable garden in the dry and dusty Plains, an oasis in the desert. Countless birds not found elsewhere on the Plains assemble here in summer, beautifying with song and bright plumage all the green, cool places. Flowers of exquisite fragrance and great brilliancy of color are found. There are many varieties. In fall and spring, migratory water-fowl descend to disport themselves in the pools.

The ranch house, which still remains in excellent condition, was such a house as appealed to a man seeking shelter from winter storms or summer heat. Its original walls of adobe were boxed and plastered, giving them a thickness of nearly two feet. On its dirt floors jangled many a spur. At the kitchen door hangs the triangle gong with which the cook called the cow punchers to meals. Struck with its heavy bar of iron, this old gong booms and rumbles until it can be heard far out on the Plains. Each of its sides measures more than two feet.

When this region was wild and uninhabited, these springs were frequented by buffalo in enormous numbers, crowding and fighting their way to water. In the neighborhood of the pools were treacherous bogs, which at this day are a menace to live stock. In the old days buffalo must have mired there by hundreds.

Here the Indians encountered this noble game to their liking. A mile or two east of the springs, there is a slight swell in the Plains where the Comanches are said to have maintained their hunting camp when in that vicinity. From this camp the Plains could be surveyed for miles in every direction. Mounting their horses, the Indian hunters descended like thunderbolts upon the buffalo massed at the springs, and slaughtered them at will. The hides were pegged down and dried in camp and the meat hung on poles and cured in the dry, pure air for winter use. A kill could be made as often as the red hunters wished to rush to the attack.

This account of the history of Buffalo Springs has been given by Mr. John Skelley, one of the rugged and reliable pioneers of Cimarron County.

"I was at Buffalo Springs as early as 1878, when I was a boy 14 years old. At that time there were no buildings. There had been some adobes made, either by Bill Hall, of Kansas City, or Dan Taylor of Trinidad, or both, in order to build a house to shelter their winter line-riders, as a line-camp was kept at the Springs every winter. My father was a freighter at Trinidad, where I was raised, and he hauled the lumber down to Buffalo Springs from Trinidad, to cover and floor the house. I made the trip with him. This was in 1878.

"The house was never built, as the fall and winter of '78 were so cold and severe that the line-riders burned all the lumber for wood. The nearest timber was on the Currumpaw, or Beaver, about eight or ten miles northwest of the Springs, where there are still a few stunted cedars and a growth of cottonwoods.

"In 1884 the Capitol Freehold Land & Cattle Syndicate established a ranch at Buffalo Springs. This company is the one that built the capitol at Austin, Texas, for which it was paid in millions of acres of land. This ranch was stocked with cattle. I worked for the man who had the fence contract. We finished the contract in December, 1885.

"During that year the owners had put in about 20,000 head of cattle, brought from the south. Better grass could not be found anywhere. A few mustangs and buffalo were still left in the country, but disappeared from that vicinity in 1887. Stragglers could be found around Company M water as late as 1889. This water was six or eight miles southeast of the present town of Boise City, the county seat of Cimarron County, Oklahoma.

"In the fall of 1885 a big prairie fire broke out and swept the country bare from the Beaver south almost to the South Canadian. We fought it with all our strength, but there were not men enough in the country to get it under control. This misfortune was followed by an early and severe winter. The company at Buffalo Springs drifted its herds out to the Canadian and to the south Plains, yet despite every precaution the loss was tremendous. I was told that only 7,000 head

of the 20,000 were gathered the following spring.
"The company did not jump the game, but went
ahead next year. Old man Boyce, who was killed
by Sneed, was general manager of the company for
a good many years, and built up a fine ranch. A
man named Campbell was the first manager at
Buffalo Springs, followed by an Englishman
named Maud. After these came Boyce, who took
the outfit about 1890.

"The timber that is growing at Buffalo Springs
was planted by the company, and is not a natural
growth. I know of no natural timber south of
there until the Canadian is reached, though the
company has set out several tracts in timber, and
there is now lots of water in wells on their holdings
between Buffalo Springs and the Canadian.

"In the old days when we left Buffalo Springs
and traveled southeast we found no live water
until we got to the head of the Rita Blanco, about
fifty miles distant, and ten or twelve miles southeast of the present town of Dalhart. There was
and still is water at what we used to call the Perico
waterholes, some ten or twelve miles south of the
Ranch, but this water has neither source nor outlet,
as it rises and then sinks again, the Perico gradually
vanishing in the Plains.

"The Springs was a great hunting ground for
buffalo. In the fall of 1878 the valley was alive
with buffalo and mustangs, and when I was there
in that year I saw several hunters' camps. A long
time ago I talked to old Mexicans who told me

that they hunted buffalo at the Springs when they were boys. They said that expeditions of both Mexicans and Navajoes came from the settlements on the Rio Grande, in New Mexico, to procure their winter's meat.

"There was an old trail leading to the Springs from New Mexico, thence to Agua Frio, and on down through the country to the eastward. We used to call this the Old Buffalo Trail. I have not seen it in more than twenty-five years, but am told that it has become so overgrown with grass that it has almost disappeared. When I was there as a boy there were thousands of antelope on the Plains; now most of them are gone. The Forth Worth & Denver City railroad company began running its trains through the company's big estate in the spring of 1888, which hastened the disappearance of the game."

We camped overnight at Buffalo Springs, and next day followed Agua Frio, or Coldwater, which is a dry stream with occasional water holes. After proceeding about thirty miles, we saw that the stream was bearing too far to the north, so we turned south and struck the brakes of the Big Blue, a tributary of the South Canadian. This was a new country to all of us, and as strange to us as if we were its first visitors. We came to a pool that was alive with all kinds of fish, and in all directions deer and wild turkeys were very plentiful. With a whoop, everybody voted unanimously to go into camp at this place.

As a fisherman I never had any luck. Leaving this sport to the rest of the outfit, I mounted my horse, and set out to explore the surrounding country. In roaming around, I reached an abandoned Mexican camp on one of the prongs of the Blue. It had been untenanted for years. I was told by older hunters that the Mexicans used to come here every fall to kill buffalo, bringing pack trains. They remained until they got a winter's supply of meat, drying the meat and rendering the tallow.

I rejoined the outfit and we kept moving until we reached the South Canadian, crossing this stream at a point near where the LX Ranch was afterwards located. Further south, we struck Palo Duro Canyon below the waterfalls. This was a dry stream, and we were compelled to rely upon melted snow for ourselves and stock. We crossed Mulberry Creek at its head waters, and camped there several days.

After crossing the Canadian, we began seeing signs of Mexican hunters, the spots where they had camped the preceding fall being plainly visible. Shifting our course more to the northeast, we crossed the head tributaries of Salt Fork and North Fork of Red River, coming back to the Canadian about twenty miles above where Canadian City, Texas, now stands.

During all this wandering we had not seen a white man, nor a human being of any kind—only a vast wilderness, inhabited by game—truly the hunter's paradise. When we saw Red River we thought that it certainly must be the South Canadian, being misled by the fact that both were sandy streams and both dry at that time. We could see a difference between the two, however, when we got to the Canadian.

CHAPTER VI

HUGGING the south side of the Canadian, we followed an old trail, called the Fort Smith and Ford Bascom Trail, up to White Deer Creek, a beautiful, clear-running stream, fringed abundantly with timber. Right opposite the mouth of this stream, on the north side of the Canadian, are the old ruins of the original Adobe Walls, though at the time we were ignorant of this fact, and passed without halting at this historic place.

Crossing to the north side of the Canadian, we reached Moore's Creek, and were delighted to find that all along the Canadian, every four or five miles, were running streams of fine water. All the streams were timbered, some more heavily than others, and in the branches of the tall cottonwoods wild turkeys roosted by thousands, while deer and antelopes in great herds grazed in the grassy bottoms.

On Bugbee Creek we passed a camp where a white man named Wheeler had been killed that fall (1873) by Indians. The brush along the creeks was alive with quail, and we could see signs of fur animals, such as beaver, mink and otter. I was now going over ground that I should see again, but little did I dream of what the future would be.

We left the river at Moore's Creek, and went north until we struck the Palo Duro again, below where we had crossed it on our way down. Here we found quite a number of buffalo hunters camped for the winter.

Our object in making this trip was to locate a good buffalo range for the following summer. Our reason for going at this time of year was that there would be less danger of being molested by Indians, as the latter did not travel in winter, if they could avoid it, preferring the idleness and pleasure of a warm winter camp, well supplied with buffalo meat. Occasionally, however, a party of young bucks, thirsty for glory in taking scalps, would brave the cold weather and make a raid. After lying around camp with the boys on the Palo Duro for several days, we headed for our old camp on the Cimarron, where we found ourselves short of supplies, and continued on to Dodge City.

In making this big circle to Buffalo Springs, Red River, the ruins of Adobe Walls and back to Dodge City, we saw very few buffalo; only now and then would we run across a bunch of old bulls. However, there were signs everywhere showing where thousands had been herding together, and we felt certain that they would come back to their old range in the spring.

It was sometime in February, 1874, when we

got back to Dodge. We had seen enough to satisfy us that the thing to do would be to go down on the Canadian as soon as the weather settled. While waiting, we went out northwest of Dodge on my old hunting grounds. This was the last hunting I ever did north of the Arkansas. My face was set toward the forbidden country, where the Indians were looking for the scalps of white men.

In the latter part of March, 1874, I went into Dodge City, and there I met up with a lot of buffalo hunters who had come to town to get away from the lonesomeness, and have a good time. There was lots of talk about the increasing scarcity of buffalo on the old range, and all of us agreed that we would have to drift further south to make buffalo-hunting a paying business.

Those of us who had been venturing down in the Panhandle country described what we had seen, and gave our opinion of the region as a buffalo range, which, of course, was favorable.

In Dodge City at this time was a man named A. C. Myers, in the general merchandise business, who had once been a buffalo-hunter, and had built a smoke-house on Pawnee Fork, where he cured buffalo hams for eastern markets. The meat was prepared for smoking by taking the two hind quarters and dividing each into three chunks, which made six pieces of boneless meat, each about the size of an ordinary pork ham. Myers sugar-cured each piece, smoked it, and sewed it in canvas. This kind of buffalo meat was the choicest, and commanded a high price on the market. Only a few dealers cured their meat in this way.

All the hunters assembled at Dodge were convinced that never again would there be a big run of buffalo that far north, because of the enormous slaughter on that part of their range in 1872 and 1873. Our determination to drift south was opposed somewhat by the handicap of being so far from a hide market. Myers solved this question by deciding to take his outfit and stock of merchandise and pull down into the good buffalo country, somewhere on the Canadian. We had no definite point in view, expecting to locate our camp where grass, timber, water and buffalo most abounded.

Myers was quick to see that a big decline in the buffalo trade at Dodge was at hand, and was willing to take the risk of going with us to get our trade. We did not think much about it at the time, but had we calmly discussed what was ahead of us, all would have seen that the undertaking was not without peril to life. We were leaving such protection as there was in the garrisoned country and plunging into a solitude through which we would have to fight our way, if attacked, or die at the hands of hostile Indians, an enemy that inflicted the most horrible forms of death imaginable, should the victim be captured alive. There would be no

getting away by making a fast run to Fort Dodge
or Fort Hays; it meant fighting to the last ditch,
and victory to the strong.

Myers' plan was that every hunter that wanted
to go should load his wagons with supplies, such
as were used on the buffalo range, for which Myers
would pay a liberal freight rate, and upon estab-
lishing a permanent camp Myers would sell the
supplies to the hunters at Dodge City prices. This
seemed fair enough. Myers owned two teams and
wagons. The organizing of this expedition caused
much enthusiasm among the hunters at Dodge, and
many wanted to go along.

About this time James Hanrahan, a typical
frontiersman, who hunted buffalo on a large scale,
came to town. Hearing of the trip we were planning, Hanrahan decided to take his whole outfit
and go with us. This was a good boost, as we were
delighted to welcome every new-comer, especially
a man like Hanrahan, who had lots of nerve and
knew all the ins and outs of frontier life.

Soon every man was busily engaged in gathering his equipment for the long trip to the new
country. There were many things to do, and to
forget any necessary part of an outfit would cause
annoyance and trouble, as we would be far from
a railroad. We had no idea when we would get
back to civilization. A lot of fellows at Dodge
thought that maybe we might never get back.
They narrowly missed making a good guess.

Three or four days before we were ready to bid

farewell to Dodge, there came from the east a stranger named Fairchild—his first trip to this rendezvous of the buffalo-hunter, the bull-whacker and the "bad" man. Naturally, Fairchild was regarded as a "'tenderfoot."

Fairchild was wildly ambitious to plunge head over heels into the stormy life of the frontier. When he heard of our expedition, he shouted for joy, and made arrangements to go along.

My first glimpse of Fairchild made me finger my sights, for he certainly looked like game. He was arrayed in a shining broadcloth suit, a "plug" hat, a flower-bed vest. and a cravat that resembled a Rocky Mountain sunset. That he might behold the sights of Dodge in proper fashion, he had hired a livery horse, equipped with a "muley" saddle, and was riding up and down the streets, as if he owned the whole town. His get-up was so unusual in Dodge that it caused much talk and laughter.

If the raiment of the East was imposing and spectacular, that of the West was far more overpowering when assembled by a man like Fairchild. The day before we pulled out I saw him again, but hardly knew him. He had jumped from the extreme East to the extreme West, and at a single bound. He was attired in a bangup brown ducking suit, high-heeled boots, and spurs that rolled along like cart-wheels. His white sombrero was wide enough for an umbrella. Round his neck was a bandana more brilliant than a Cheyenne pony painted for the warpath. His belt was full of cartridges, and sticking from holster and scabbard were a six-shooter and a butcher knife, fearful and murderous-looking weapons. In his hands, with the air of a gay cavalier, he bore a big "50" rifle, for which he had paid the considerable sum of $85. The boys had primed him to buy the butcher knife in the belief that he needed something of the kind to scalp Indians when he slew them far, far from their homes in the forest.

There was every indication that Fairchild was well supplied with money. He came from Illinois and belonged to a good family, was well educated, and had been admitted to the bar. But he yearned for western adventure, and abandoned his profession to satisfy his chief and burning ambition. It was impossible that such a man could escape ceaseless banter in a crowd like ours.

However, Fairchild was not more delighted than myself when the day of departure came. In scouting the country, I had seen that big money could be made by a good hunter; I was not without confidence in my marksmanship. When we moved out of Dodge there were about fifty men and thirty wagons. Each man had provided himself with a saddle horse. I was never without one —the best that money could buy in that country.

All the wagons were heavily loaded, which compelled us to drive at easy stages. We got to Crooked Creek the first day out of Dodge. There was never a happier lot of men in the world. All were in rugged health, none in need, most of them inured to the hardships of life in the wilderness, each confident that he could take care of himself, sure of the help of his comrades in any emergency, and everybody as merry and jolly as could be. If there was care of any kind, it was too light to be felt. We ate like wolves, and could have digested a dry buffalo hide with the hair on. Spring was on the way, and the air was light and buoyant, making the days and nights an endless delight.

The youngest of our party was "Bat" Masterson, who was to win a reputation not only as a member of this expedition, but, later on, as gunman and journalist. It seems remarkable that finally Masterson should wander as far east as New York City and become a newspaper writer. He was a chunk of steel, and anything that struck him in those days always drew fire. In age, I was perhaps next to Masterson, being now in my twenty-fourth year.

Best of all, when we camped at night, there would be singing, dancing, music and telling of tales. In the party were a number of veterans of the Civil War, with endless stories of desperate battles that were greatly to our liking. After we had eaten heartily, and the camp-fire was aglow and crackling under the stars, some fellow would stretch and peg down a dry buffalo hide on which the men would dance turn about or in couples. The hide gave a much better footing for dancing than might be supposed, and was stiff enough and hard enough to respond in the liveliest way to jigging. There were always fiddlers in a crowd like ours, perhaps an accordeon, and a dozen fellows who could play the French harp. The scene was picturesque and pleasing. Round us rolled the interminable Plains, arched by the glittering sky, and in the fire-light the rollicking buffalo hunters sang and danced. There were no night sounds in this vast silence, save those of our camp or the yelping of coyotes and howling of wolves, disturbed by this strange invasion of their prowling ground.

It was agreed that every man in the party should do something for the entertainment of his companions at these gatherings round the campfire—dance, sing a song or tell a story. There was no dodging, we had to come across. As I never danced, wasn't much of a talker, and couldn't possibly sing, all this was hard on me. I did my best, however, even trying to learn to play a fiddle, which had been given to me by a friend at Hays City. But there was no music in me—I couldn't scratch out "Dan Tucker." Long afterward, when I was married and my oldest daughter developed a talent for music, I was greatly pleased, though aware of the fact that she had inherited none of it from me.

Drinking in the pure fresh air of the Plains, we rolled from our blankets every morning, clear-headed and ready for any enterprise. Just to feel one's self living in that country was a joy. We heard nothing and cared nothing about politics; it made little difference to us who was president of the United States; we worked hard, had enough money for our common needs, and were happy, happier perhaps than we ever were in later years. Youth probably had much to do with our contentment.

The second day's travel brought us to the Cimarron River, and here we stopped at one of my old camp-grounds. We had reached the "dead line"—beyond was hostile Indian country.

I am moved here to say something about the Cimarron. This stream rises in New Mexico, and after passing through the northeastern corner of that State, it nips off a small part of the southeast corner of Colorado and passes into the State of Kansas. After a bend to northward, it flows south into that part of Oklahoma once known as "Neutral Strip," or "No Man's Land," jogs back into Kansas between Clark and Comanche counties, and then turns for the last time into Oklahoma, where it pursues a generally southeast course until it meets the Arkansas River in the central part of the state. Cimarron is a Spanish word, meaning "outcast, outlaw, or wanderer," a name sometimes applied in Spanish-speaking countries to a steer that wanders away from the herd and ranges alone, wild and intractable. The word also means "big-horn," and was probably given by early Spaniards because of the big-horn or mountain sheep that in early days ranged about the head of the Cimarron River.

The Cimarron is true to its name. Though born of white mountain snows, its waters soon become red and turbid. In Oklahoma the Cimarron crosses several large expanses of salt, making its water undrinkable; in fact, so much salt is held in solution that a large swallow of the water is sufficient to produce nausea. The bed of the Cimarron in the Plains or prairie country is flat and sandy, though at rare intervals it has rugged shores. Throughout a greater portion of the year, the volume of water to be seen by the eye is small, the current crawling snake-like along its sandy waste. Rarely, however, is the Cimarron without a perceptible current, and usually this current has a rapid flow.

The Cimarron is commonly regarded as one of the most dangerous streams in the southwest. Its width often is three or four hundred yards. If there were no sand, the stream would be rather imposing in size. It is filled to the brim with sand, however, and through the sand is an underflow. The quicksands of the Cimarron are notorious. No crossing is ever permanently safe. The sand grips like a vise, and the river sucks down and buries all that it touches—trees, wagons, horses, cattle and men alike, if the latter should be too weak to extricate themselves. In the old days countless buffaloes begged down and disappeared beneath the sands of the Cimarron. Their dismembered skeletons are frequently uncovered at this day when the river is in flood.

After a rise, the Cimarron is peculiarly dangerous. As it boils and rolls along, the river loosens and hurls forward an astonishing quantity of sand. Unless naked, a man quickly finds himself pulled down by the increasing weight of sand that lodges in his clothes, and swimming becomes difficult, and finally impossible save with tremendous exertion. Stripped bare, a swimmer can sustain himself in the Cimarron with greater ease than in most other streams, as the salt and sand give the water extraordinary buoyancy. No man should ever tackle the Cimarron in flood until after he has stripped to the skin and kicked off his boots. The experienced cow-pony seems to realize its danger when crossing the Cimarron, taking short, quick steps, and moving forward without the slightest pause. To stop would be to sink in the quicksand.

The Cimarron is subject to sudden and dangerous floods, floods that seem to come from nowhere. In central Oklahoma, for example, weeks may pass without a drop of rain. A settler crosses the river at noon, blinded by the clouds of sand that have been whipped up by the wind, and finding the water scarcely reaching his horses' knees. Fifteen minutes later he returns to the crossing, and finds the river roaring and thundering from bank to bank. What is known as a "head rise," formed by a cloud-burst far out in the Plains country, has come down, a solid wall of water often four or five feet in height. Sometimes two or more of these "head rises" follow each other in succession. The sand is torn loose and brought up from the very bottom of the river. To venture into the Cimarron at such times would be folly. If it must be crossed, the safest way is to ride a horse that knows how to handle himself in a flood of this kind. If the rider can swim it is usually best for him to seize his horse's tail and follow behind. The safest thing to do is to stay on dry land until the flood has passed, and then sound the crossing. The latter can be made firm by driving a herd of cattle back and forth, which causes the sand to precipitate and begin packing, soon forming a bar.

The Salt Fork of the Arkansas and the South Canadian are counterparts of the Cimarron in the dangers they oppose to travelers and live stock.

After crossing the Cimarron without difficulty, we held a conference on the Indian problem, as discretion and prudence now impelled us to proceed with caution. It was agreed that if we should encounter Indians and find them manifesting friendship we would do likewise. This was their country, we argued, and if they would leave us alone, we would be willing to leave them alone.

Ever since we had left Dodge City, Fairchild had been eager to get into an Indian fight, and had bragged about what he would do when the time came. He said that he would not allow an Indian to do or say the least thing to him without his killing the Indian. He was bad medicine from the forks of the creek, a wolf with hydrophobia, a blizzard in July.

We fully understood the fact the Fairchild did not realize how much trouble a break on his part might bring to the whole outfit. We really feared that he might fire up on a peaceable Indian, and cause all of us to be massacred.

So it was thought best by several practical jokers among us to take time by the forelock in provoking to action the blood-thirsty Fairchild. We waited until we had reached the South Canadian before dosing out the medicine to him.

Fairchild loved to hunt, and would ride away from the outfit nearly every day after deer and antelope. Some of the men had made Fairchild believe that he could kill an antelope at a distance of two miles, and he would blaze away as far as he could see them. By "scratch" shots, Fairchild managed to kill several antelope and he swelled up with pride until he was almost unrecognizable. What finally happened to him will be told later.

After leaving the Cimarron, we crossed "No Man's Land." In the brakes of the Cimarron we had the hardest kind of pulling, as there was lots of sand and the country was rough. The fourth day brought us to the Beaver, the main prong of the North Canadian, its other branch being Wolf Creek. Both the Beaver and Wolf Creek unite at Camp Supply, the point to which I had helped haul supplies for the Custer expedition, with the outfit of mules that stampeded in harness as we were returning to Fort Hays.

This time we struck the Palo Duro at its mouth, where there was plenty of water. Here we camped and then moved into the Panhandle of Texas. Now we began striking camps of buffalo-hunters who had prepared to stay on the Plains during the winter. They were as glad to see us as we were to find them. The coming of more hunters made everybody feel more secure, if there should be an outbreak by the Indians.

In one of these camps were Fred Singer, who now lives in Dodge City, and two Englishmen, Jim and Bob Cator, both of whom I had met at Hays City, Kansas, in 1870, when they had just arrived from England, and were still wearing knee breeches and buckles. Their togs attracted a great deal of attention. The Cators became close friends of mine in later years. Bob went to Oregon, and Jim settled on the Palo Duro, in Hansford County, where he now runs a cow ranch close to where he was camped at the time of which I write. Bob Cator was the first postmaster in Hansford County, and when the latter was organized he was elected county judge, holding the office a number of years. Jim and Bob Cator named Dixon Creek, in Hutchinson County, in remembrance of the fact that I built a dugout and was the first man to camp on this creek in 1874.

After I went away, they occupied the dugout. This creek still bears my name.

After the Cators had settled on the Palo Duro, two brothers, a sister and Jim Cator's sweetheart came out from England and joined them. They could scarcely have gone to a more remote place, and the change from England to the Panhandle country, as they found it at that time, must have been startling. Jim married his sweetheart at Dodge City. Having business at Granada, he took his bride along; the boys teased him about his "wedding" trip. Both the young women were refined and highly educated. Miss Cator was an accomplished horsewoman, one of the best I ever saw. She taught school for several years and then married Clate McCrea. She is still living in Hansford County.

Determined that we would keep moving until we found the best buffalo country, we went south from the Palo Duro and struck Moore's Creek at its source, following this stream to the South Canadian River, where we camped about two miles below the present town of Plemons.

Here we were disappointed at not finding the grass better; there was hardly enough grass for our stock. I am convinced that a number of the Panhandle streams are gradually changing. I clearly recall that Moore's Creek then was a narrow, swift-running stream, and that at almost any point a man could jump across it. Since that day, Moore's Creek has been frequented by great herds of cattle which trample its sandy shores until wind and rain have flattened its once steep banks and given the stream a width of several hundred yards. A like change has come to most of the smaller streams that flow into the South Canadian in the Panhandle country.

In this camp on the South Canadian we paid our respects to Fairchild. All liked him, but he was so bent upon killing an Indian that we felt something must be done, as we were not down in that country to hunt Indians. Though severe, the dose had to be administered. Of course, everybody save Fairchild knew what was going on.

In a large grove of cottonwoods just above our camp hundreds upon hundreds of wild turkeys roosted every night. When a turkey hunt was proposed, to take place at night, Fairchild grew so eager and excited to go that he could scarcely control himself.

Three men were selected to slip quietly out of camp and at a certain place in the timber have a fire burning when the hunting party got there. One of them came back to serve as guide. Ostensibly he was to lead the hunters to the best and biggest roost, but actually he was to pilot them to the immediate vicinity of the fire.

Fairchild was so impatient to start that it was difficult to persuade him to wait until darkness had fallen and the turkeys had settled to roost.

I do not believe it would have been possible to

find a man who loved practical joking more than did "Bat" Masterson. He was in his glory at that sort of thing, and was forever pulling off something of the kind. "Bat" was one of the three that had gone out to build the fire. He now came to camp, ready to pilot the hunters where they would "sure find a million turkeys"—and the camp-fire.

It was arranged that "Bat" should start out, with Fairchild close at his heels and Myers bringing up the rear. "Bat" cautioned Fairchild to keep both eyes wide open and to move softly, as the turkeys must not be frightened.

Rounding a bend of the creek, where the timber was dark and dense, the hunters suddenly found themselves slap-bang against a camp-fire in full blaze. "Bat" motioned to Fairchild to move back into the timber. The three then held a consultation to discover, if possible, who had built the fire. "Bat" was dead sure that it was an Indian camp; he had been dreaming about Indians two or three nights he said, and was now fearful that the worst was at hand. Myers tried to argue that "Bat" was mistaken and rattled, if not actually showing a streak of yellow; anyway, he was willing to bet that Fairchild could whip all the Indians in the Panhandle if given a fair show.

Bang! Bang! Bang! Half a dozen shots were fired in the direction of the hunters. The bullets whistled and ripped through the branches close above their heads. Myers took the lead back to camp, yelling bloody murder at every step, to terrify Fairchild. "Bat" came last, gradually dropping behind and firing his six-shooter until Fairchild was confident that the most desperate fight with Indians imaginable was at hand.

"Run, Fairchild; run for your life!" shouted Masterson.

At a bound Fairchild had passed Myers, and tore into camp like a tornado coming through a forest. He was half a mile ahead of "Bat" and Myers. They had led him far enough away to give him a long, hard run.

Fairchild stumbled and fell exhausted on a pile of bedding, gasping for breath, his eyes distended and his teeth chattering. We crowded round, seemingly in great alarm, asking him a thousand questions about the cause of his fright. For several minutes he was unable to speak, and acted as if he were suffocating. Finally, he managed to say in a hoarse whisper:

"Injuns."

"Oh, men, he must be shot," exclaimed a mischievous hunter.

Thereupon, another joker seized a butcher knife and ripped Fairchild's shirt down the back from collar to tail. Another, frantically calling for water, and finding none, emptied the contents of the camp coffee pot down Fairchild's bare back, which alarmed Fairchild with the fear that he had been wounded.

Fairchild was recovering by the time Myers and

Masterson and the men who had been at the camp-
fire bounded in, panting for breath, and began up-
braiding Fairchild for abandoning them to the
mercy of the Indians. We had asked Fairchild
what had become of "Bat" and Myers, and
he feebly replied:

"Killed, I guess."

"How many Indians were there, and did you
see them?"

He answered that he did not know how many
there were, because of the way they shot, but he
was sure that the timber was full of them. Once
he heard something whiz past his head which he
knew was not a bullet, but an arrow.

Masterson now stepped forward and tremblingly
declared that the whole turkey roost country
was alive with Indians. Instantly, there was rushing to and fro in preparation for defense. Serious,
perhaps fatal trouble for everybody, was at hand;
the devil was to pay and no pitch hot. All kinds
of suggestions were offered as to what was best
to do. Some of the boys were in favor of starting
at once for Dodge City, as the Indians would be
unable to follow our trail at night, and we might
get far enough away by daylight to escape. Fairchild was firmly committed to the Dodge City
plan.

More resolute men were in favor of fighting it
out, if every man bit the dust, and proposed that a
strong guard be thrown round the camp, and that
the men take turns standing guard until morning.

This plan was adopted, and the guards were stationed at regular intervals everywhere round camp, save on the river side, where a high bank offered protection against sudden surprise.

Fairchild was placed on guard nearest the river, and warned to maintain a vigilant lookout along the edge of the bank, as the Indians might swim up the river and plug him when he wasn't looking, after which they could kill everybody in camp. As a matter of fact, it would have been impossible for the enemy to approach in this manner, because of the swiftness of the water, and the banks were too high and steep to be scaled.

By this time Fairchild was ready to believe anything he heard and was so badly rattled that he failed to see that we had left our camp-fire burning, something that we would never have done had we actually felt that Indians were in the vicinity, as fires would have exposed us to a broadside from the darkness. Fairchild was in no frame of mind to think of trifles, and obeyed all orders without asking why.

The guards were stationed, and shortly afterward, one by one, they came in, all save Fairchild, who stood at his post. There was much noisy laughter over the trick we had played on him. When Fairchild failed to meet the next guard, he became suspicious, and drew near camp, where he overheard what we were saying. Then he came in, with blood in his eyes. I have often thought that he was the angriest man I ever saw in my

life. We were too many for him, or else he would
have crippled somebody. He refused to eat breakfast, and sulked for several days. This cured him,
however, of wanting to kill an Indian, and ever
afterwards he was a good hunter and a good
fellow.

The last time I saw Fairchild he had his sleeves
rolled up, skinning buffalo, and on his face was a
coat of tan half an inch thick. He bore little re-
semblance to the tenderfoot I had first seen at
Dodge City.

Fairchild was not the only fellow we treated
in this manner. The boys delighted in playing
jokes upon each other. The worst scare I ever got
was in 1870 when I was working for a man near
Fort Hays. He owned a herd of beef cattle which
he had sold to the Government. One day three of
us were out with the herd. The cattle had been
stampeding practically every day, and we were
having lots of trouble with them.

We were riding along the Saline River, looking
for strays. Campbell, a member of the outfit, was
a quarter of a mile behind Thompson and myself.
Campbell suddenly emptied his six-shooter and
dashed toward us, shouting "Indians!" at the top
of his voice. He knew that he was mounted upon
a much swifter horse than either of ours, and
passed us like the wind.

Thompson and I looked back, but could see no
signs of Indians. We were certain, nevertheless,
that Campbell was in earnest. We put both spurs

to our horses and rode after him at top speed. The country was very rough, and we supposed that after Campbell and the Indians fired at each other, the Indians had dropped behind a ridge. We felt that we were making a run for our lives. Campbell was going so fast that we could not overtake him. Occasionally, he would stop long enough for us to come within speaking distance, whereupon he would shout, "Hurry up; there they come!" and dash away.

He kept this up for about four miles. Our objective point was a wood-choppers' camp, where we expected to make a stand against the Indians. If we were killed, we could at least die among men of our own race. We were hopeful, however, of being able to beat the Indians off.

Our horses were now in a lather, and rapidly breaking down. Rounding a little knoll, we saw Campbell lying on the ground and rolling from side to side, as if in acute pain. Perhaps he had been shot. Upon reaching him, we found to our inexpressible rage and disgust that his paroxysms were caused by laughter—he said that he had not seen an Indian all that day; just wanted to play a trick on us. We made Campbell swear not to tell the other boys; he kept his word.

CHAPTER VII

WE had lots of fun sky-larking in our camp on Moore's Creek, but spring was coming on, and it was our wish to establish a permanent camp at the best possible place. Unconsciously, we were drawn to that place as other men, long, long before us, had been drawn. We reached it by pulling right down the river bottom about twelve miles to what was then called West Adobe Walls Creek but which is now called Bent Creek.

It is a beautiful stream, clear and swift. About a mile from its mouth stood the old ruins of the original Adobe Walls. Here we stopped and camped for the night. We had heard of these ruins ever since we had been in the Plains country. They were of great interest to us, and we carefully examined them, wondering what men in such a far-off day had ventured to establish themselves here, and why they had done so. We were not acquainted with the history of the place. We thought of Mexicans and different Indian tribes of the Southwest. As a matter of fact, there are the remains of villages and old burial grounds on Wolf Creek in the Panhandle which men who claim to know about such things declare are the remains of the easternmost extension of the Pueblo civilization. I have no opinion in the matter.

When we first saw Adobe Walls, there were parts of walls still standing, some being four or five feet high. The adobe bricks were in an excellent state of preservation. Many different stories have been told about this place and its origin. While I was hunting buffalo in southern Kansas I met up with a man named Charley Powell who had been a soldier in the Third Cavalry. He told me that in 1863, when they were going from Fort Smith, Arkansas, to Fort Bascom, New Mexico, the trail lay on the south of the Canadian, opposite Adobe Walls. The soldiers crossed over and looked at the ruins. Even at that time none of the buildings was standing.

Later, when I was serving as scout at Fort Elliott, Texas, I was talking with General John P. Hatch one day, and we fell to discussing the Adobe Walls country. He told me that he passed up the Canadian in 1848 with the regiment of Mounted Rifles, going out west, and stopped to examine these ruins. He said that only the broken walls were to be seen and that there was much to indicate that the place long since had been abandoned. On this expedition he was a second lieutenant; at the time I talked with him he was lieutenant colonel of the 4th United States Cavalry, and in command at Fort Elliott, an old, gray-haired man. He was shrewd and very industrious. He took pride in improving Fort Elliott, and had a mania for using adobe bricks in the erection of buildings. Employing Mexicans, who were past masters in the making of these bricks, Colonel Hatch built stables large enough to hold horses for three troops of cavalry. He put up so many adobe buildings at Fort Elliott that finally he was called "Doby" Hatch.

It is probable that old Adobe Walls was built by Colonel William Bent, in the first 40's or earlier, the year 1844 being possible. Colonel Bent's son, George Bent, now living at Colony, Okla., made this statement :

"Bent & Company built Adobe Walls, as it is called. I cannot find out when it was built. It was a trading post to trade with the Comanches, Kiowas and Prairie Apaches. Bent & Company traded for horses and mules from the Indians. They sent their traders in summer time to trade for this stock. The post was not occupied in winter, as the Company did not trade for buffalo robes, as the trading post was too far from Bent's Fort on the Arkansas River to haul the hides. These horses and mules were driven to Missouri and sold; also, to the Platte Rivers, to be sold to the emigrants. The Comanches, Kiowas and Apaches were rich in horses and mules. They stole many in old Mexico and traded off the wild ones very cheap. Bent & Company employed many Mexicans to break these wild animals, after which the latter were sold to the whites."

The noted plainsman and Indian trader, John Smith, told George Bent that together with five or six companions he made his escape from old Adobe Walls, after it had been attacked by Comanches and Kiowas.

Even though it be true that old Adobe Walls was established by Colonel William Bent and his associates, a tradition remains that they merely seized upon a site that had been occupied at an even earlier day by men of whom nothing is known, save that they are believed to have come from the Spanish settlements in New Mexico. There are traditions of buried treasure at Adobe Walls, and strangers have appeared there in search of it. One of these treasure-hunters was an old gray-haired man who came after the country had been settled. His story was that a pack train loaded with gold and silver bullion had been attacked at this place by Indians. In its extremity, the besieged party buried the bullion. Only one or two members of the expedition escaped massacre, among the slain being a Catholic priest.

The old man in search of the treasure was too feeble to do the physical work of digging, and tried to hire men to work for him. He was looked upon as slightly demented, and could get no assistance. He departed without finding the buried fortune. Subsequently, his story was revived, and men living in the locality made numerous excavations, but found nothing.

The day after we camped on Bent Creek, several of the boys rode northeast, to look over the country. Upon their return, they reported that there was an excellent site for a permanent camp on the next creek, about a mile and a half further on; so we pulled up the valley and began unloading our wagons on the bare ground in a broad valley where there was a pretty stream called East Adobe Walls Creek. This was to become a spot memorable to all of us.

Myers & Leonard built a picket house twenty by sixty feet in size. James Hanrahan put up a sod house, twenty-five by sixty, in which he opened a saloon. Thomas O'Keefe built a blacksmith's shop of pickets, fifteen feet square. Thus, a little town was sprouting in the wilderness—a place where we could buy something to eat and wear, something to drink, ammunition for our guns, and a place where our wagons, so necessary in expeditions like ours, could be repaired.

While all this hammering and pounding and digging was going on, I started with three companions and rode the country as far down as where the present town of Clarendon, Texas, now stands. We were absent about fifteen days, and upon our return we found the buildings about finished. We did not see many buffalo on this trip. Maybe the buffalo had scented Indians. We ranged as far east as Cantonment Creek, and on its east prong encountered a few scattering bulls. The season was too early for the cows and bulls to begin mating and running together.

On Cantonment Creek we stopped at some seeping springs. A lone cottonwood stood tall and

gaunt among a few hackberries. I cut my name on
this lone tree. One of the men who was with me
at that time was a Frenchman, for whom we had
no other name than "Frenchy," just as we had
single names for many other men in the Plains
country. He was an excellent cook, and I always
thought he could broil buffalo steak better than any
other man I ever knew.

In returning to camp, we crossed Red Deer
about where Miami, Texas, now is, and camped at
some water-holes. Heading northward we soon
struck the brakes of Tallahone, and followed the
Tallahone down to its mouth. This was a timbered
creek with an abundance of running water. Perch
and catfish were so plentiful that enough to feed
the whole camp could be caught in a few minutes.
Deer and wild turkeys were in sight all along
the Tallahone, and there were numerous signs of
beaver and otter.

Here we crossed the Canadian at what for many
years was the main crossing in this part of the
country, and followed along the north side of the
river to Adobe Walls.

During our absence from camp, Rath & Wright
came down from Dodge City with another outfit
and built a sod house sixteen by twenty feet. This
firm bought buffalo hides and was engaged in general merchandising. The business was in charge of
James Langton.

The buildings were finished as rapidly as possible, and every man at Adobe Walls who could be

induced to engage in this kind of manual labor was given a job and paid well for his services. Each building had a big cottonwood ridge log upon which the upper end of each of the rafter poles rested. The poles were covered with dirt and sod. For safety and convenience in handling their stock, Myers & Leonard built a stockade corral. This enclosure was made by setting big cottonwood logs in the ground. The logs were hauled across the Canadian, from Reynolds Creek, a distance of about six miles, a laborious undertaking.

I had no liking for the monotony and restraint of camp life and was impatient to be about my own business, which was to find a good buffalo range and begin hunting. After remaining in camp two days, we saddled and mounted again, to go up the Canadian as far west as Hell's Creek. We crossed the river and followed the old Fort Bascom Trail to Antelope Creek, where we crossed over to the Arroyo Bonito, on which the LX Ranch afterwards established headquarters. The Arroyo Bonito is one of the prettiest streams in the Panhandle country, with a good flow of water and lots of timber.

Here I struck the trail I had made during the the previous winter, and I now followed it back across the Canadian and thence north to Grapevine Creek, where I camped two or three days. This was at the edge of the Plains. At intervals all along the way we struck small bands of bulls. Buffalo were surprisingly scarce. Sometimes we killed them, and at other times did not molest them. Generally, there were from four to ten in a bunch. The scarcity of buffalo rather discouraged us, and we redoubled our efforts to locate a big herd. We held to the east, keeping along the edge of the Plains and coming down to the Canadian between Bugbee Canyon and Big Creek. Bugbee Canyon received its name from the fact that Thomas Bugbee settled there in 1877. His was one of the first cow ranches established in the Panhandle of Texas. Charles Goodnight, whom I met first in the fall of 1875, brought his cattle a year later from Colorado to Palo Duro Canyon. Mrs. Goodnight joined her husband soon afterwards.

We were in the Bugbee Canyon country in May, 1874. The season was delightful. The air was fresh and invigorating, the grass was green, flowers were blooming, the sky was clear, the sunshine pleasant, and a feeling of joy and happiness was everywhere. Those were splendid nights, out there under the stars. The mornings came with dazzling splendor. At this season sunrise on the Plains presented a scene of magnificence. I always had the feeling that it came with a thunderous sound.

When we struck Big Creek I noticed a patch of lamb's quarter (wild greens), and I told the boys we would go into camp and cook a pot of greens, which we did. We ate greens to our hearts' content.

Searching out every point in the country, next day we followed an old trail down to the Canadian valley, striking it at a high point, afterward known as Dixon's Point, on account of its being opposite Dixon's Creek. We soon reached Adobe Walls.

All the buildings had been finished, and everybody was doing a good business. Quite a number of hunters had come down from the north, and a plain trail had been opened between Adobe Walls and Dodge City, a hundred and fifty miles away. Freight outfits were making regular trips between the two places.

All of the hunters acquainted with the habits of the buffalo knew that the herds would soon be coming north from the region where they had spent the winter. The spring had been unusually late, which held back the buffalo in their migration. There was nothing for us to do but wait until the buffalo were moved by that strange impulse that twice annually caused them to change their home and blacken the Plains with their countless, moving forms. We could lie around camp or vary the monotony by going to Adobe Walls and joining in the fun that was rampant at that place. Our amusements were mostly card-playing, running horse-races, drinking whisky and shooting at targets, the latter to improve our marksmanship.

All this soon got old to me, and about the last of May I pulled out again. Crossing the Canadian at the mouth of White Deer Creek, I followed the latter to its head and went out on the Plains, keeping along their edge until I came to Dixon Creek. Here I found an ideal camping place, with plenty of wood, grass and water. I decided to build our permanent camp, and was soon industriously at work. I knew by the signs that buffalo had been through here, and it was certain that they would soon be coming back.

I had two men with me, "Frenchy," whom I employed as a skinner, and Charley Armitage, an agreeable fellow who had come from England. Those Englishmen certainly loved the life of the frontier.

We had been here two or three days when the expected happened. Getting up one morning earlier than my companions, I chunked the fire for breakfast, and stood waiting for it to begin blazing. Then a familiar sound come rolling toward me from the Plains—a sound deep and moving, not unlike the rumbling of a distant train passing over a bridge. In an instant I knew what was at hand. I had often heard it. I had been listening for it for days, even weeks.

Walking out on a high point near camp, I gazed eagerly toward the horizon. I could see nothing save the vast undulating landscape. My ears, however, had revealed to me what my eyes could not see. The buffalo were coming!

Hurrying back to camp, I shouted the good news to Armitage and "Frenchy," rousing them from their sleep and telling them to hurry breakfast. They lost no time in making coffee, frying meat and browning a cake of bread. I saddled my horse by the time breakfast was ready, and after eating hurriedly I sprang into my saddle and went south at a gallop.

After I had ridden about five miles, I began striking small bunches of buffalo bulls, all headed north and all moving. A further ride of eight miles carried me out on the Plains. My muscles hardened and grew warm at the sight. As far as the eye could reach, south, east and west of me there was a solid mass of buffalo—thousands upon thousands of them—slowly moving toward the north.

The noise I had heard at early daybreak was the bellowing of the bulls. At this time of year— the breeding season—the bellowing of the countless bulls was continuous, a deep, steady roar that seemed to reach to the clouds. It was kept up night and day, but seemed to be deepest and plainest at early morning.

I was happy beyond measure, and turned my horse toward camp, hastening at full speed to let my men know what I had found. Already, the buffalo were approaching the vicinity of my camp, and in sight of it I shot thirty-five or forty, all bulls; the boys were soon busily at work with their skinning knives. By night buffalo were passing within gunshot of our camp.

Business had now begun in earnest, and we would soon be enjoying a steady income, to offset our winter's expenses. Where buffalo were as plentiful as they were here I could easily kill enough in a day to keep ten skinners busily at work. I killed enough next day to keep "Frenchy" and Armitage employed for several days, and went down to Adobe Walls in a light wagon, to see if I could hire more skinners. I found one man who would go with me, but for only a few days, until his partner should return with a load of hides. All the other hunters had heard the good news, and had pulled out for the buffalo range. Adobe Walls was deserted, save for the merchants and their clerks. By offering this man twenty-five cents a hide for skinning, I induced him to go with me for a week or ten days.

On my way I had undertaken to pick out the most direct route from my camp to Adobe Walls. Keeping on the divide between Dixon Creek and Short Creek, I came to a stretch of very rough country late in the evening, and finally reached a place where it was impossible to travel further in a wagon. As darkness was falling, I unhooked my mules, Tobe and Joe, and jumped astride old Tobe, followed some buffalo trails down to Dixon Creek, near its mouth, where grass and water were abundant.

As this particular locality was new to me and darkness at hand, I decided that I would camp there for the night. Picketing one of the mules, I turned the other one loose. With a single blanket for my bed and my coat for a pillow, I lay down for the night, and was soon sound asleep.

No mercy was shown the buffalo when I got back to camp from Adobe Walls. I killed as many as my three men could handle, working them as hard as they were willing to work. This was deadly business, without sentiment; it was dollars against tenderheartedness, and dollars won.

When the man I had hired at Adobe Walls had worked his full time, I hitched up and started back with him. When we reached the Canadian we found her with her back up, smashing and banging things from side to side—so deep and swollen that it would have been the height of foolishness to attempt a crossing. We went on to White Deer Creek, hoping to find a wider crossing, and by reason of it a shallower bottom.

I waded the river in my search for a good footing, and decided finally that we could cross by swimming the mules fifty or sixty yards. It was our purpose to unhitch the mules and leave the wagon on the south side of the river until the water had run down.

Our plans were quickly changed. At that moment two men from Adobe Walls rode up and told us that two hunters had been killed by Indians twenty-five miles down the river, on Chicken Creek, several days past. Our informants were greatly excited, and were hurrying back to their camp at the head of White Deer.

If the Indians were on the warpath, we knew it would be foolish to leave our wagon, as they would destroy it beyond doubt; so we decided to risk trying to take it across the river regardless of the wide stretch of rolling water.

While men experienced in the trials of travel in the wilderness may grow indifferent to danger, yet they never forget that danger exists. This is especially true in crossing such streams as the South Canadian and the Cimarron. These streams make the odds in their own way and in their own favor. The man that ventures into them must rely solely upon his own nerve, strength and horse sense.

Choosing a point on the opposite side of the river where we wished to land, we drove in, hoping for the best. In a moment the swift current caught us, and both mules were swimming. In water a mule has less sense than a horse, and the ginger is soon knocked out of him if he gets his ears full of water. Having smaller feet, the mule cannot equal a horse in traversing quicksand.

After the mules had taken a few plunges, the current caught up our wagon and whirled it over and over like a top. When I saw that the mules would have to swim for it, I sprang into the water to help the frightened animals, getting on their upper side and seizing the mule nearest me by his bridle. In this way I was able to keep his head above water. The other mule, terrified by its surroundings, alternately rose and sank. We saw that if the wagon kept turning over, the team might get drowned; so we cut the harness, and after the greatest exertion got the mules ashore. The near mule lay down on the sand and died without a struggle. It seemed ridiculous that the mule should succumb after being taken from the water, yet there he lay. Old Tobe was saved. The wagon drifted down stream about sixty yards and lodged against the bank. We pulled it out of the river next day. Our greatest misfortune was the loss of our guns.

When we lined up on the north side of the river we were a sorry lot—two bedraggled, unarmed men and a water-logged mule three miles from Adobe Walls, in danger of attack by Indians at any moment. Ordinarily, I was not easily discouraged. This, however, was a jolt from the shoulder. I stood in greatest need of my gun, a big "50." We could dig out the wagon, but not the guns, and somewhere in the depths of the Canadian they are rusting this very day.

We were a sorrowful pair as we started up the valley for Adobe Walls, leading old Tobe and leaving old Joe to bleach on the Canadian sands. Old Joe had led me out of the country infested with mosquitoes and I was still grateful. Unwilling to let the other walk, neither of us would ride. I had lost my hat in the river, and my clothing was plastered with mud and sand.

Upon coming in sight of Adobe Walls, we were quickly discovered, and our disordered appearance convinced the men that we had been attacked by Indians—possibly we were the only survivors of a desperate encounter. We found Adobe Walls buzzing with talk about Indians. The particulars of the killing of the men on Chicken Creek were now learned. Their names were Dudley and Wallace. They were camped on the west side of the creek near where the Ledrick brothers now have a ranch. Dudley, Wallace and Joe Plummer were hunting together from this camp. Plummer went to Adobe Walls for supplies. Upon his return he was horrified to find the dead bodies of his two companions. Through the breast of one had been driven a heavy wooden stake, pinning him to the ground. Both were scalped, and otherwise multilated in a shocking manner.

Looking away from his camp, Plummer said he saw objects at a distance which he felt sure were Indians. Realizing that the next thing for him to do was to try to save his life, he cut the harness from one of his horses, mounted and dashed away toward Adobe Walls.

The news he brought caused much excitement, as these were the first men that had been killed since the building of Adobe Walls. When Plummer reached the Walls there were only a few men there, but he managed to get two buffalo-hunters to go back with him to bury the dead. A party of fifteen surveyors, employed by the State of Texas, and in charge of a man named Maddox, had just arrived in that section. I am told that this was the first surveying ever done in the Panhandle, and that the Maddox survey still holds good. The surveyors' camp was on Johns' Creek. Plummer had halted there on his way to Adobe Walls, to warn the men against the Indians.

When Plummer returned, the members of the surveying party joined him to help bury the dead. No further indignities had been offered the bodies, which were buried on the spot. The horses, still in their harness, were found grazing in the valley. Plummer gathered up the outfit and went to Adobe Walls—the surveyors kept going straight south, fully satisfied that soldiers, not surveyors, were what the country most needed.

Hearing all this, I was impatient to return to my own camp as quickly as possible, but was detained by the necessity of buying a mate for my mule, but nobody had a mule to sell. Finally, I managed to buy a horse. My next obstacle to overcome was to replace the gun I had lost in the Canadian. The best I was able to do was to buy what was called a round-barrel Sharp's. I had left camp in such a hurry that I failed to take my six-shooter, an oversight of which I was rarely guilty in those days. I had been absent three days when I got back to my camp.

The evening before I left Adobe Walls, another hunter came in with Indian news. His name was Moore. He said that two days previously two men had been killed by Indians in his camp on a tributary of Salt Fork of Red River, north of where Clarendon, Texas, is now situated. The names of the dead men were John Jones, nicknamed "Cheyenne Jack," a young Englishman, and "Blue Billy," a German. The camp was destroyed and all the stock run off.

"Cheyenne Jack" belonged to an influential family in England. His relatives, several years later, made inquiry through the British diplomatic service, in communication to the commanding officer at Fort Elliott, Texas, as to the whereabouts of the unfortunate man's remains. I was directed to find where the body had been buried. It was a week after Moore reported these murders before a party went from Adobe Walls to bury the dead men. Jones and his companion had fallen in the bed of a creek in a grove of timber, right in camp. While Moore was absent, a flood came down the creek and carried the bodies and the whole camp away. The bodies could not be found.

Before leaving the Walls to go to my camp, I got "Brick" Bond, now living at Dodge City, Kansas, to accompany me. I was fearful that the Indians had attacked my camp and possibly killed Albright and "Frenchy." Happily, I found them alive and ignorant of what had been going on in the country south of the Walls.

All of us agreed that a blind man could see that it was entirely too risky to stay in camp with Indians all around us; so we lost no time in loading our outfit and pulling into Adobe Walls, arriving there by noon the next day. The story of the Indian depredations had spread to all the hunting camps, and by the time we reached the Walls a large crowd had gathered in from the surrounding country. We remained here for about a week.

An odd thing about this Indian excitement was that none of the hunters had seen an Indian nor a sign of one. The Indians evidently had carefully picked their time, watching closely and waiting until only two or three men were in camp, whereupon they attacked and then slipped stealthily away. All of us felt that these murders had been perpetrated as a warning to the buffalo-hunters to leave the country—to go north of the "dead line."

Every man of us was dead set against abandoning the buffalo range. The herds were now at hand, and we were in a fair way to make big money. Furthermore, the buffalo were becoming scarcer and scarcer each year, and it was expedient that we make hay while the sun shone, for soon the sun would be no longer shining in the buffalo business. Its night was close at hand. We decided that the best and safest plan would be for three or four outfits to throw in together and all occupy the same camp. After all, it was not unusual to hear of two or three buffalo-hunters being killed and scalped every year, and perhaps there would be no further outbreaks by the Indians. It was agreed, however, that everybody should be very careful and take every precaution against surprise and attack.

When we started back to the range, most of us went west and north of the Walls, as the Indians were supposed to be camped on the headwaters of the Washita and the Sweetwater, south of us, their main summer camp grounds. But I was so in love with my location on Dixon Creek, southwest of the Walls, that I resolved to take the risk and establish myself at that point, and went there with three skinners I had hired.

We had left a lot of hides at this camp, and began hauling them to Adobe Walls, which took several days. I felt uneasy all the time. Something seemed to be wrong. There was Indian in the air, and I could not shake myself loose from thinking about the possible danger; so I told my men that it might be well for us to get over on the north side of the Canadian. We broke camp and went to Adobe Walls, to increase our stock of supplies for a stay near the head of Moore's Creek.

We were buying supplies to last us two months, and were ready to start next day. Late in the evening James Hanrahan came to me and said:

"Billy, where are you going?"

"Northwest," I answered.

Hanrahan then asked me how it would suit me for the two of us to throw in together. He said he had been having trouble in getting a man who could hunt fast enough to keep his skinners busy. Hanrahan owned a big outfit, and usually had seven skinners. I told him that nothing would please me more than to go into partnership with him, and that I could easily kill enough buffalo to keep twenty skinners hard at work every day. Hanrahan offered to give me half of all the profits, which was as liberal as any man could wish for.

Our wagons were all assembled and loaded, in readiness for us to pull out next morning, June 27, 1874.

It might be well to describe the exact location of the buildings and the nature of their surroundings. All the buildings at Adobe Walls faced to the east, the main ones standing in a row. On the south was the store of Rath & Wright, with a great pile of buffalo hides at the rear. Then came Hanrahan's saloon, and fifty yards or so north of the latter was the store of Myers & Leonard, the building forming the northeast corner of the big picket stockade. In the southwest corner of the stockade was a mess house, and between the mess house and the store was a well. The blacksmith's shop was located just north of Hanrahan's saloon.

The adobe walls of the main buildings were about two feet thick. The door of Rath & Wright's store opened to the west, while that of Myers & Leonard looked to the east.

Bent's Creek, west of the Walls, flowed from the northwest in a southeasterly direction to the Canadian, passing close to the ruins of old Adobe Walls, about a mile and a quarter south of the new Adobe Walls. On the north side of the Bent's Creek, southwest of the buildings, was a hill, north of which the land was smoother and afterward a part of the Turkey Track Ranch pasture.

East of Adobe Walls lay the open valley of Walls Creek, terminating in a growth of willows, cottonwoods, hackberry and chinaberry that fringed this stream, on the other side of which, at a distance of about twelve hundred yards from Myers & Leonards' store, stood a butte-like hill of considerable height, with a more or less level bench near the summit, caused by the sliding and falling of debris from the crest. Several hundred yards southeast were the low sandhills of the Canadian, whose wide expanse of level sand was more than a mile away.

The season had advanced so slowly, and the buffalo had been so long coming north, that we had done comparatively little hunting, and all of us were impatient to be up and gone. O'Keefe was doing a big business at his blacksmith's shop, pounding away hour after hour, repairing the wagons on which the buffalo hides were to be hauled from the hunting grounds to the traders at Adobe Walls. My wagon was in front of the shop, O'Keefe having finished repairing it.

I had been unable to replace my big "50," lost in the Canadian, with a gun that suited me in every way, but it was highly important that I should be well-armed if I expected to fulfill my promises to Hanrahan.

The only gun at the Walls that was not in use was a new "44" Sharp's, which was next best to a "50." This gun had been spoken for by a hunter who was still out in camp; he was to pay $80 for it, buying it from Langton, who was in charge of Rath & Wright's store. Langton told me that if nec-

essary he would let me have the gun, as he had
ordered a case of guns and was expecting them to
arrive any day on the freight train from Dodge
City, and he probably would have them in stock
before the owner of the gun came in from the
buffalo range. News came in that night, the evening of June 26, 1874, that the freight wagons were
camped on the flats north of the Walls and, of
course, would show up in a day or two. Langton
also heard that the man to whom he had promised
the gun was not coming for several days, so he
hunted me up and told me I might have the gun.

I went right over to his store and got the "44,"
together with a full case of ammunition. I was so
tickled over my good luck, that I took the gun over
to Hanrahan's saloon, to show it to him. After we
had looked the gun over, I set it down in the corner
for the night, intending to get it when we said
good bye to the Walls next morning, headed for
our camp on the buffalo range. For some reason
which I can not explain, even to myself, I left the
case of ammunition with Langton, little dreaming
how greatly I would regret my carelessness.

By this time the excitement and talk about the
fate of the four men who had been killed by Indians had subsided, and we paid no further attention to the matter, so busily were we engaged in
our preparations for departure. Several hunters
had come in that day, and we planned to stay up
late that night, celebrating our return to the range,

telling stories of past experiences and joking about how much money we would have when the hunt was over.

The night was sultry and we sat with open doors. In all that vast wilderness, ours were the only lights save the stars that glittered above us. There was just a handful of us out there on the Plains, each bound to the other by the common tie of standing together in the face of any danger that threatened us. It was a simple code, but about the best I know of. Outside could be heard at intervals the muffled sounds of the stock moving and stumbling around, or a picketed horse shaking himself as he paused in his hunt for the young grass. In the timber along Adobe Walls Creek to the east owls were hooting. We paid no attention to these things, however, and, in our fancied security against all foes frolicked and had a general good time. Hanrahan did a thriving trade.

CHAPTER VIII

ON that memorable night, June 26, 1874, there were twenty-eight men and one woman at the Walls. The woman was the wife of William Olds. She had come from Dodge City with her husband to open a restaurant in the rear of Rath & Wright's store. Only eight or nine of the men lived at the Walls, the others being buffalo-hunters who by chance happened to be there. There was not the slightest feeling of impending danger.

As was the custom in the buffalo country, most of the men made their beds outside on the ground. I spread my blankets near the blacksmith's shop, close to my wagon. I placed the gun, the "round barrel" Sharp's, by my side between my blankets, as usual, to protect it from dew and rain. A man's gun and his horse were his two most valuable possessions, next to life, in that country in those days.

Every door was left wide open, such a thing as locking a door being unheard of at the Walls. One by one the lights were turned out, the tired buffalo-hunters fell asleep, and the Walls were soon wrapped in the stillness of night.

Late that evening I had gone down on the creek and caught my saddle horse—a better one would have been hard to find—and tied him with a long picket rope to a stake pin near my wagon.

About 2 o'clock in the morning Shepherd and Mike Welch, who were sleeping in Hanrahan's saloon, were awakened by a report that sounded like the crack of a rifle. They sprang up and discovered that the noise was caused by the cracking of the big cottonwood ridge pole.

This ridge pole sustained the weight of the dirt roof, and if the pole should break the roof would collapse and fall in, to the injury or death of those inside. Welch and Shepherd woke up a number of their companions to help them repair the roof. Some climbed on top and began throwing off the dirt, while others went down to the creek to cut a prop for the ridge pole.

This commotion woke up others, and in a little while about fifteen men were helping repair the roof. Providential things usually are mysterious; there has always been something mysterious to me in the loud report that came from that ridge pole in Hanrahan's saloon. It seems strange that it should have happened at the very time it did, instead of at noon or some other hour, and, above all, that it should have been loud enough to wake men who were fast asleep. Twenty-eight men and one woman would have been slaughtered if the ridge pole in Hanrahan's saloon had not cracked like a rifle shot.

By the time we had put the prop in place, the

sky was growing red in the east, and Hanrahan asked me if I did not think we might as well stay up and get an early start. I agreed, and he sent Billy Ogg down on the creek to get the horses. Some of the men, however, crawled back into bed. The horses were grazing southeast of the buildings, along Adobe Walls Creek, a quarter of a mile off.

Turning to my bed, I rolled it up and threw it on the front of my wagon. As I turned to pick up my gun, which lay on the ground, I looked in the direction of our horses. They were in sight. Something else caught my eye. Just beyond the horses, at the edge of some timber, was a large body of objects advancing vaguely in the dusky dawn toward our stock and in the direction of Adobe Walls. Though keen of vision, I could not make out what the objects were, even by straining my eyes.

Then I was thunderstruck. The black body of moving objects suddenly spread out like a fan, and from it went up one single, solid yell—a warwhoop that seemed to shake the very air of the early morning. Then came the thudding roar of running horses, and the hideous cries of each of the individual warriors who engaged in the onslaught. I could see that hundreds of Indians were coming. Had it not been for the ridge pole, all of us would have been asleep.

In such desperate emergencies, men exert themselves almost automatically to do the needful thing. There is no time to make conscious effort, and if a man loses his head, he shakes hands with death.

I made a dash for my saddle horse, my first thought being to save him. I never thought for an instant that the oncoming Indians were intending an attack upon the buildings, their purpose being, as I thought, to run off our stock, which they could easily have done by cutting in ahead of them. I overlooked the number of Indians, however, or else I might have formed a different opinion.

The first mighty warwhoop had frightened my horse until he was frantic. He was running and lunging on his rope so violently that in one more run he would have pulled up the stake pin and gone to the land of stampeded horses. I managed to grab the rope, and tie my horse to my wagon.

I then rushed for my gun, and turned to get a few good shots before the Indians could turn to run away. I started to run forward a few steps. Indians running away! They were coming as straight as a bullet toward the buildings, whipping their horses at every jump.

There was never a more splendidly barbaric sight. In after years I was glad that I had seen it. Hundreds of warriors, the flower of the fighting men of the southwestern Plains tribes, mounted upon their finest horses, armed with guns and lances, and carrying heavy shields of thick buffalo hide, were coming like the wind. Over all was splashed the rich colors of red, vermillion and ochre, on the bodies of the men, on the bodies of the running horses. Scalps dangled from bridles, gorgeous war-bonnets fluttered their plumes, bright feathers dangled from the tails and manes of the horses, and the bronzed, half-naked bodies of the riders glittered with ornaments of silver and brass. Behind this head-long charging host stretched the Plains, on whose horizon the rising sun was lifting its morning fires. The warriors seemed to emerge from this glowing background.

I must confess, however, that the landscape possessed little interest for me when I saw that the Indians were coming to attack us, and that they would be at hand in a few moments. War-whooping had a very appreciable effect upon the roots of a man's hair.

I fired one shot, but had no desire to wait and see where the bullet went. I turned and ran as quickly as possible to the nearest building, which happened to be Hanrahan's saloon. I found it closed. I certainly felt lonesome. The alarm had spread and the boys were preparing to defend themselves. I shouted to them to let me in. An age seemed to pass before they opened the door and I sprang inside. Bullets were whistling and knocking up the dust all around me. Just as the door was opened for me, Billy Ogg ran up and fell inside, so exhausted that he could no longer stand. I am confident that if Billy had been timed, his would have been forever the world's record. Billy had made a desperate race, and that he should escape seemed incredible.

We were scarcely inside before the Indians had surrounded all the buildings and shot out every window pane. When our men saw the Indians coming, they broke for the nearest building at hand and in this way split up into three parties. They were gathered in the different buildings, as follows:

Hanrahan's Saloon—James Hanrahan, "Bat" Masterson, Mike Welch, Shepherd, Hiram Watson, Billy Ogg, James McKinley, "Bermuda" Carlisle, and William Dixon.

Myers & Leonard's Store—Fred Leonard, James Campbell, Edward Trevor, Frank Brown, Harry Armitage, "Dutch Henry," Billy Tyler, Old Man Keeler, Mike McCabe, Henry Lease, and "Frenchy."

Rath & Wright's Store—James Langton, George Eddy, Thomas O'Keefe, William Olds and his wife, Sam Smith, and Andy Johnson.

Some of the men were still undressed, but nobody wasted any time hunting his clothes, and many of the men fought for their lives all that summer day barefoot and in their drawers and undershirts.

The men in Hanrahan's saloon had a little the best of the others because of the fact that they were awake and up when the alarm was given. In the other buildings some of the boys were sound asleep and it took time for them to barricade the doors and windows before they began fighting. Barricades were built by piling up sacks of flour and grain, at which some of the men worked while others seized their guns and began shooting at the Indians.

The number of Indians in this attack has been variously estimated at from 700 to 1,000. I believe that 700 would be a safe guess. The warriors were mostly Kiowas, Cheyennes and Comanches. The latter were led by their chief Quanah, whose mother was a white woman, Cynthia Ann Parker, captured during a raid by the Comanches in Texas. Lone Wolf was a leader of the Kiowas, and Stone Calf and White Shield led the Cheyennes.

For the first half hour the Indians were reckless and daring enough to ride up and strike the doors with the butts of their guns. Finally, the buffalo-hunters all got straightened out and were firing with deadly effect. The Indians stood up against this for awhile, but gradually began falling back, as we were emptying rawhide saddles entirely too fast for Indian safety. Our guns had longer range than theirs. Furthermore, the hostiles were having little success—they had killed only two of our men, the Shadler brothers who were caught asleep in their wagon. Both were scalped. Their big Newfoundland dog, which always slept at their feet, evidently showed fight, as the Indians killed him, and "scalped" him by cutting a piece of hide off his side. The Indians ransacked the wagon and took all the provisions. The Shadlers were freighters.

At our first volleys, a good many of the Indians

jumped off their horses and prepared for a fight on foot. They soon abandoned this plan; and for good reason. They were the targets of expert rough-and-ready marksmen, and for the Indians to stand in the open meant death. They fell back.

The Indians exhibited one of their characteristic traits. Numbers of them fell, dead or wounded, close to the buildings. In almost every instance a determined effort was made to rescue the bodies, at the imminent risk of the life of every warrior that attempted this feat in front of the booming buffalo-guns. An Indian in those days would quickly endanger his own life to carry a dead or helpless comrade beyond reach of the enemy. I have been told that their zeal was due to some religious belief concerning the scalp-lock—that if a warrior should lose his scalp-lock his spirit would fail to reach the happy hunting grounds. Perhaps for the same reason the Indian always tried to scalp his fallen enemy.

Time and again, with the fury of a whirlwind, the Indians charged upon the building, only to sustain greater losses than they were able to inflict. This was a losing game, and if the Indians kept it up we stood a fair chance of killing most of them. I am sure that we surprised the Indians as badly as they surprised us. They expected to find us asleep, unprepared for an attack. Their "medicine" man had told them that all they would have to do would be to come to Adobe Walls and knock us on the head with sticks, and that our bullets would

QUANAH PARKER

not be strong enough to break an Indian's skin. The old man was a poor prophet.

Almost at the beginning of the attack, we were surprised at the sound of a bugle. This bugler was with the Indians, and could blow the different calls as cleverly as the bugler on the parade ground at Fort Dodge. The story was told that he was a negro deserter from the Tenth Cavalry, which I never believed. It is more probable that he was a captive halfbred Mexican that was known to be living among the Kiowas and Comanches in the 60's. He had been captured in his boyhood when these Indians were raiding in the Rio Grande country, and grew up among them, as savage and cruel as any of their warriors. How he learned to blow the bugle is unknown. A frontiersman who went with an expedition to the Kiowas in 1866 tells of having found a bugler among them at that time. The Kiowas, he said, were able to maneuver to the sound of the bugle. This bugler never approached the white men closely enough to be recognized.

Somebody soon discovered that the Indian warriors were charging to the sound of the bugle. In this they "tipped" their hand, for the calls were understood, and the buffalo-hunters were "loaded for bear" by the time the Indians were within range. "Bat" Masterson, recalling this incident long after the fight, said:

"We had in the building I was in (Hanrahan's saloon), two men who had served in the United States army, and understood all the bugle calls.

The first call blown was a rally, which our men instantly understood. The next was a charge, and that also was understood, and immediately the Indians come rushing forward to a fresh attack. Every bugle call he blew was understood by the ex-soldiers and was carried out to the letter by the Indians, showing that the bugler had the Indians thoroughly drilled.

"The bugler was killed late in the afternoon of the first day's fighting as he was running away from a wagon owned by the Shadler brothers, both of whom were killed in this same wagon. The bugler had his bugle with him at the time he was shot by Harry Armitage. Also he was carrying a tin can filled with sugar and another filled with ground coffee, one under each arm. Armitage shot him through the back with a 50-caliber Sharp's rifle, as he was making his escape."

Billy Tyler and Fred Leonard went into the stockade, but were compelled to retreat, the Indians firing at them through the openings between the stockade pickets. Just as Tyler was entering the door of the adobe store, he turned to fire, and was struck by a bullet that penetrated his lungs. He lived about half an hour after he was dragged into the store.

The Indians were not without military tactics in trying to recover their dead and wounded. While one band would pour a hot fire into the buildings other Indians on horseback would run forward under the protection of this fusilade. They suc-

STONE CALF AND WIFE
Algonquin Family, Southern Cheyenne Tribe

ceeded in dragging away a good many of the fallen.

Once during a charge I noticed an Indian riding a white horse toward where another Indian had gone down in the tall grass. The latter jumped up behind the Indian on the horse, and both started at full speed for safety. A rifle cracked and a bullet struck the horse. We could see the blood streaming down the horse's leg. Both Indians began whipping the poor brute and, lurching and staggering on three legs, he carried them away.

Along about 10 o'clock, the Indians having fallen back to a safer distance from the buffalo-guns, some of us noticed a pony standing near the corner of a big stack of buffalo hides at the rear of Rath's building. We could see that an Indian behind the hides was holding the pony by the bridle, so we shot the pony and it fell dead. The pony was gaily decorated with red calico plaited in its name.

The falling of the pony left the Indian somewhat exposed to our fire, and the boys at Hanrahan's and Rath's opened upon him full blast. They certainly "fogged" him. No Indian ever danced a livelier jig. We kept him jumping like a flea back and forth behind the pile of hides.

I had gotten possession of a big "50" gun early in the fight, and was making considerable noise with it. I sized up what was going on behind the pile of buffalo hides, and took careful aim at the place where I thought the Indian was crouched. I shot through one corner of the hides. It looked to me as if that Indian jumped six feet straight up into the air, howling with pain. Evidently I had hit him. He ran zig-zag fashion for thirty or forty yards, howling at every jump, and dropped down in the tall grass. Indians commonly ran in this manner when under fire, to prevent our getting a bead on them.

I managed to get hold of the "50" gun in this manner. The ammunition for mine was in Rath's store, which none of us was in the habit of visiting at that particular moment. I had noticed that Shepherd, Hanrahan's bartender, was banging around with Hanrahan's big "50," but not making much use of it, as he was badly excited.

"Here, Jim," I said to Hanrahan, "I see you are without a gun; take this one."

I gave him mine. I then told "Shep" to give me the "50." He was so glad to turn loose of it, and handed it to me so quickly that he almost dropped it. I had the reputation of being a good shot and it was rather to the interest of all of us that I should have a powerful gun.

By noon the Indians had ceased charging, and had stationed themselves in groups in different places, maintaining a more or less steady fire all day on the buildings. Sometimes the Indians would fire especially heavy volleys, whereupon wounded Indians would leap from the grass and run as far as they could and then drop down in the grass again. In this manner a number escaped.

We had no way of telling what was happening

to the men in the other buildings, and they were equally ignorant of what was happening to us. Not a man in our building had been hit. I could never see how we escaped, for at times the bullets poured in like hail and made us hug the sod walls like gophers when a hawk is swooping past.

Before long there were a large number of wounded horses standing near the buildings. A horse gives up quickly when in pain, and these made no effort to get away. Even those that were at a considerable distance from the buildings when they received their wounds came to us, as if seeking our help and sympathy. It was a pitiable sight, and touched our hearts, for the boys loved their horses. I noticed that horses that had been wounded while grazing in the valley also came to the buildings, where they stood helpless and bleeding or dropped down and died.

By noon we were running short of ammunition. Hanrahan and I decided to make a run for Rath's store, where there were thousands of rounds that had been brought down from Dodge City for the buffalo hunters. Another thing we had in mind was to get ammunition for the new gun I had bought the evening before, which would give us the use of one more gun in the saloon.

We peered cautiously outside to see if any Indians were ambushed where they could get a pot shot at us. The coast looked clear; so we crawled out of a window and hit the ground running and made a dash to Rath's in the fastest kind of time. The Indians saw us, however, before the boys could open the door, and opened at long range. The door framed a good target. I have no idea how many guns were cracking away at us, but I do know that bullets rattled round us like hail. Providence seemed to be looking after the boys at Adobe Walls that day, and we got inside without a scratch, though badly winded.

We found everybody at Rath's in good shape. We remained here some time. Naturally, Hanrahan wanted to return to his own building, and he proposed that we try to make our way back. There were fewer men at Rath's than at any other place, and their anxiety was increased by the presence of a woman, Mrs. Olds. If the latter fact should be learned by the Indians there was no telling what they might attempt, and a determined attack by the Indians would have meant death for everybody in the store, for none would have suffered themselves to be taken alive or have permitted Mrs. Olds to be captured.

The boys begged me to stay with them. Hanrahan finally said that he was going back to his own place, telling me that I could do as I thought best. Putting most of his ammunition into a sack, we opened the door quickly for him, and away he went, doing his level best all the way to his saloon, which he reached without mishap.

CHAPTER IX

I N the restaurant part of Rath's store, a transom
had been cut over the west door; this transom
was open, as no glass had even been put in. This
door had been strongly barricaded with sacks of
flour and grain, one of the best breastworks
imaginable, the Indians having no guns that could
shoot through it.

Climbing to the top of this barricade, to take a
good look over the ground west of the building, I
saw an object crawling along in the edge of the tall
grass. Levelling my gun, and taking aim with my
body resting on one knee, I fired. The recoil was
so great that I lost my balance and tumbled backward from the top of the barricade. As I went
down I struck and dislodged a washtub and a
bushel or two of cooking utensils, which made a
terrific crash as they struck the floor around me. I
fell heavily myself, and the tumbling down of my
big "50" did not lessen the uproar. The commotion startled everybody. The boys rushed forward
believing that I had been shot, even killed. I found
it quite difficult to convince them that I had not
been shot, and that most of the noise had been
caused by the tub and the tin pans.

I was greatly interested in the object I had shot

at, so I crawled up on the sacks again. By looking closely, I was able to see the object move. I now fired a second time, and was provoked at seeing the bullet kick up the dirt just beyond the object. I tried the third time and made a center shot.

By 2 o'clock the Indians had fallen back to the foot of the hills and were firing only at intervals. They had divided their force, putting part on the west side and part on the east side of the buildings. Warriors were riding more or less constantly across the valley from one side to the other, which exposed them to our fire. So we began picking them off. They were soon riding in a much bigger circle, and out of range.

This lull in the fighting was filled with a kind of disturbing uncertainty. Since early morning, we had been able to hold the enemy at bay. We were confident that we could continue to do so as long as we had ammunition. We thanked our stars that we were behind thick sod walls, instead of thin pine boards. We could not have saved ourselves had the buildings been frame, such as were commonly built in frontier towns in those days. Still, there was no telling how desperate the Indians might become, rather than abandon the fight; it was easily possible for them to overwhelm us with the brute force of superior numbers by pressing the attack until they had broken down the doors, and which probably would have been attempted, however great the individual sacrifice, had the enemy been white men. Luckily, it was impossible to set the sod on fire, or else we should have been burned alive.

Though we did not relax in watchfulness when the Indians withdrew, yet we were able to throw off some of the high tension that had kept our nerves and muscles as taut as bowstrings since day-break. A man's mouth gets dry and his saliva thick and sticky when he fights hour after hour, knowing that if he goes down his death will be one of torture, unless he should be instantly killed. All forenoon the Indians had been descending upon us like a storm, taunting us in every imaginable way, even pounding upon the doors with their guns and lances, and vying with each other in feats of martial horsemanship. They had flaunted the bloody scalps of the poor Shadlers with devilish glee. Time and again, however, we had ripped into them with our guns and brought down horses and warriors until in many places the grass around Adobe Walls was stained with blood.

About 4 o'clock in the afternoon a young fellow at Hanrahan's, "Bermuda" Carlisle, ventured out to pick up an Indian trinket that he could see from the window. As he was not shot at, he went out a second time, whereupon others began going out, all eager to find relics. For the first time, we now heard of the death of Billy Tyler at Myers & Leonard's. Tyler had been killed at the beginning of the fight, as had the Shadlers.

When I saw that it was possible to leave the buildings with reasonable safety, I determined to satisfy my curiosity about three things.

An iron-gray horse had been standing for hours not far from the south window of Hanrahan's saloon. I could not understand what had held him so long, before he was finally shot by the Indians themselves. When I reached the spot, the mystery was clear—there lay a dead warrior who had fallen in such a way as to make fast the rope that held the horse. The horse wore a silver-mounted bridle. With a buffalo bone I pried open the stiffened jaws and removed the bridle, also taking the rawhide lariat.

On the side of the bridle, about ten inches from the bit, was fastened a scalp, which evidently had been taken from the head of a white woman, the hair being dark brown in color and about fifteen inches in length. The scalp was lined with cloth and edged with beads. Several other scalps were found that day. One was on a war shield.

My attention likewise had been attracted by an object at the rear of the little sod house west of Rath's store. We had fired at it over and over until we had cut a gap in the corner of the sod house. The object finally had disappeared from sight. For a considerable time we had seen feathers whipping round the corner in the wind, and had thought that probably three or four Indians were concealed there. Every time I had turned loose my big "50" I had torn out a chunk of sod.

When I reached the sod house, I was startled at what I saw. There sat a painted and feathered warrior in a perfectly upright position with his legs crossed and his head turned to one side in the most natural way imaginable. His neck was broken and he was stone dead. I am bound to admit that I jumped back, fearful that he was alive and would bore me through and through before I could pull down on him.

What we had been shooting at so frequently was the dead warrior's lance, which was covered with webbing and adorned with black feathers at intervals of every five or six inches. The lance had been stuck upright in the ground, and had been shot in two, which caused the feathers to disappear —the upper part had doubled over across the dead Indian's legs. I added the lance to my "prizes of war."

The object that I had seen crawling along the edge of the tall grass was the third that demanded my attention. I found a dead Indian lying flat on his stomach. He was naked, save for a white breech-cloth. His six-shooter was in his belt. The Indian had been shot through the body, and one knee had been shattered. I could plainly see the trail he had made by the blood on the grass. A short distance away lay a shot pouch and a powder horn; there were about fifteen army cartridges in the pouch. A few steps farther, was his 50-caliber needle gun, an army Springfield. Next, were his bow and his quiver. I confiscated the whole outfit.

One of the noisiest and most active spectators of the fight was a young crow that some of the hunters had captured shortly after our arrival at Adobe Walls. The crow had been petted by every man in camp. All of us were acquainted with the old superstition that the crow is an omen of death. During the worst of the fight this crow flew from one building to another, in and out of the open windows, calling "Caw! Caw! Caw!" in the most dismal way. It would alight on some object in the room, and sit there calling and cawing until somebody, tiring of the noise, would shout, "Get out of here, you black rascal!" and then chase him from the building. The crow would fly to another building and repeat his performance. Despite the bullets, this crow was never injured and, save our horses, was the only thing left outside.

There were several dogs at the Walls, but all of them cut for tall timber when the fighting began and did not show up for several days. All our horses were killed or run off. The five horses that had been left in the stockade were quickly shot down, the Indians poking their guns between the cottonwood pickets. Four head tied to a wagon near Rath's were cruelly killed. I saw the Indians when they first rode up and tried to cut the rope with a butcher knife. One was a gray mare that was notorious for her vicious kicking. She would not let the Indians approach her, so all were shot. My own saddle horse, which I had owned for years and highly prized, was among the first to be shot, and still lay tied to the wagon when I found him.

The Indians were not without military strategy. They had planned to put every man of us afoot, thereby leaving us without means of escape and powerless to send for aid unless some messenger might steal away in the darkness, to traverse on foot the weary distance and the dangerous and inhospitable region that lay between us and Dodge City. By holding us constantly at bay and keeping fresh detachments of warriors rallying to the attack they probably thought it possible to exhaust our strength, and then overwhelm us. It should be remembered that Adobe Walls was scarcely more than a lone island in the vast sea of the Plains, a solitary refuge uncharted and practically unknown. For the time we were at the end of the world, our desperate extremity pressing heavily upon us, and our friends and comrades to the north ignorant of what was taking place.

At the first dash, the Indians had driven off all the horses they had found grazing in the little valley, which Billy Ogg had gone in the dusk of dawn to round up preparatory to our departure for the hunting grounds. We counted fifty-six dead horses scattered in the immediate vicinity of the buildings, some with arrows sticking in their bodies, and others bored with bullets. Of these ten head belonged to the hunters. Added to this slaughter were the twenty-eight head of oxen that belonged to the Shadler brothers. In nearly every instance, a horse that had been wounded far from the buildings would stagger in our direction, apparently to get as close as possible to his friends. There they would stand in agony until the Indians shot them down, leaving none alive.

The last victim of their cruelty was a mustang colt owned by Mrs. Olds. This colt had been captured by some of the hunters among a bunch of wild mustangs, and given as a present to Mrs. Olds, who had petted the graceful, affectionate little creature until it followed her from place to place like a dog. Some rather romantic stories have been written about this mustang colt and the part it played in the fight at Adobe Walls. The truth, however, unadorned, is that the colt remained near the buildings throughout the fight, and when I saw it a feathered arrow was sticking in its back. I never knew whether the colt died of this wound or was afterwards shot to put the poor little thing out of its misery.

When we found that we could move around outside the buildings without danger of immediate attack, we blanketed the bodies of Tyler and the Shadlers and dug a single grave near the north side of the corral. There they lie to this day, without a stone to mark the spot. Many a spring and many a summer have come and gone, and many a winter has sent its blinding snows across the Panhandle since that far-off day. The Indians and the buffalo have vanished from the scene, and the plow is running over the land where they ranged. After all, the boys are sleeping as quietly and as restfully as if they had been buried in the village churchyard back at their old homes.

Despite the utmost efforts of our savage foes to carry away their dead and wounded, thirteen dead Indians were left on the ground near the buildings, so closely under the muzzles of our guns that it would have been suicide for their comrades to have attempted their recovery. By the time we had buried our three comrades, darkness had come, and we abandoned further outside work and returned to the protection of the buildings, completely exhausted by the strain and excitement of the day's fighting.

What we had experienced that day ate into a man's nerves. I doubt if any of us slept soundly that June night. Somewhere out there in the darkness our enemies were watching to see that nobody escaped from the beleagured sod buildings. Inasmuch as Indians rarely, if ever, attack at night, preferring the shadows of early morning when sleep is soundest, and when there is less chance of their being ambushed, we felt reasonably certain of not being attacked before daybreak. As for myself I dreamed all night, the bloody scenes of the day passing in endless procession through my mind; I could see the Indians charging across the valley, hear the roar of the guns and the blood-curdling war-whoops, until everything was a bewildering swirl of fantastic colors and movements.

All my comrades at Adobe Walls that day

showed much courage. It is with pride that I can recall its many incidents without the feeling that there was the slightest inclination on the part of any man to show the "white feather." To be nervous or fearful of death is no sign of weakness—sticking at one's post and doing the thing that is to be done is what counts.

"Bat" Masterson should be remembered for the valor that marked his conduct. He was a good shot, and not afraid. He has worked his way up in the world, and has long been a successful writer for a New York newspaper. He was sheriff of Ford County, Kansas, at Dodge City, in 1876-77. It has always seemed strange to me that finally he should prefer life in a big city, after having lived in the West. I have been told that he said that he had no wish again to live over those old days, that they no longer appealed to him, but I never believed it. Such a psychology is contrary to human nature.

All that long night after the first day's fighting not a sound was heard nor did an Indian come near. Next morning the pet crow was the only living object to be seen in the valley, where he was holding high carnival on the dead horses, flying from one carcass to another.

By this time such an awful stench was rising from the dead Indians and dead horses that we were forced to get rid of them. As we had no teams with which to drag them away, we rigged up several buffalo hides and tied ropes to them, then rolled the bodies onto the hides and pulled them far enough away to prevent the evil smell from reaching the buildings. In this way three or four men could move a horse.

At one place, between Rath's and Hanrahan's, twelve horses lay piled together. We dug a pit close at hand and rolled them in. The other horses and the Indians were dragged off on the prairie and left.

On the second day we saw only one bunch of Indians. They were on a bluff across the valley east of us. Some of our men opened up on them at long range; the Indians returned the fire and disappeared. It was plain to them that there was still a lot of fight left in us.

Our situation looked rather gloomy. With every horse dead or captured, we felt pretty sore all around. The Indians were somewhere close at hand, watching our every movement. We were depressed with the melancholy feeling that probably all the hunters out in the camps had been killed. Late that afternoon our spirits leaped up when we saw two teams coming up the valley from the direction of the Canadian. This outfit belonged to George Bellfield, a German who had been a soldier in the Civil War.

A black flag was flying from one of the buildings, and when Bellfield and his companions saw it they thought we were playing some kind of joke on them. In broken English Bellfield remarked to his men, "Dem fellers tink dey's damn smart, alretty." But when he drew nearer and began seeing the dead horses, he put the whip to his team and came in at a dead run.

When asked if they had been attacked by Indians, Bellfield and his men said that they had not seen a sign of one. That same day Jim and Bob Cator came in from their camp north of Adobe Walls.

It was of greatest importance that somebody should go to Dodge City for help. Henry Lease, a buffalo hunter, volunteered to undertake this dangerous journey, Bellfield furnishing a horse. Lease started after dark on the second day. He carefully examined his pistols and his big "50," filled his belts with plenty of ammunition, shook hands with us and rode away in the night. I doubt if there was a man who believed that Lease would get through alive. It was a certainty, however, that there would be a pile of dead Indians where he fell, if he were given a fighting chance for his life.

At the same time we sent out two men to visit the different camps, and warn the hunters that the Indians were on the war path. They were to bring back the news if the hunters were dead.

On the third day a party of about fifteen Indians appeared on the edge of the bluff, east of Adobe Walls Creek, and some of the boys suggested that I try the big "50" on them. The distance was not far from seven-eighths of a mile. A number of exaggerated accounts have been written about this incident. I took careful aim and pulled

High Bluff East of Adobe Walls on Which Billy Dixon Killed an Indian at 1538 Yards.

the trigger. We saw an Indian fall from his horse. The others dashed out of sight behind a clump of timber. A few moments later two Indians ran quickly on foot to where the dead Indian lay, seized his body and scurried to cover. They had risked their lives, as we had frequently observed, to rescue a comrade who might be not only wounded but dead. I was admittedly a good marksman, yet this was what might be called a "scratch" shot.

More hunters came in on the third day, and as news of the Indian outbreak spread from camp to camp the boys were soon coming in like blackbirds from all directions—and they lost no time making the trip. By the sixth day there were fully a hundred men at the Walls, which may have given rise to the statement so frequently made in after years that all these men were in the fight.

The lone woman who was at Adobe Walls, Mrs. Olds, was as brave as the bravest. She knew only too well how horrible her fate would be if she should fall into the hands of the Indians, and under such circumstances it would have caused no surprise had she gone into the wildest hysterics. But all that first day, when the hand of death seemed to be reaching from every direction, this pioneer woman was cool and composed and lent a helping hand in every emergency.

By the fifth day enough hunters had arrived to make us feel comparatively safe, yet it was expedient that we should protect ourselves as fully as possible, so the men began fortifying the buildings.

None of them had been finished, nor had any port-holes been cut in the walls. Our shooting was done from the windows and transoms. With port-holes we could have killed many more Indians. A little enclosure with sod walls was now built on top of Rath's store, and another on top of Myer's for look-outs. A ladder led from the inside to these lookouts.

On the fifth day William Olds was stationed in the lookout on Rath's store, to watch for Indians while the other men were at work. The lookout on the other buildings shouted that Indians were coming, and all of us ran for our guns and for shelter inside the buildings. Just as I entered Rath's store I saw Olds coming down the ladder with his gun in his hand. A moment later his gun went off accidentally, tearing off the top of Old's head. At the same instant Mrs. Olds rushed from an adjoining room—in time to see the body of her husband roll from the ladder and crumple at her feet, a torrent of blood gushing from the terrible wound. Olds died instantly. Gladly would I have faced all the Indians from the Cimarron to Red River, rather than have witnessed this terrible scene. It seemed to me that it would have been better for any other man there to have been taken than the husband of the only woman among us. Her grief was intense and pitiable. A rough lot of men, such as we were, did not know how to comfort a woman in such distress. We did the best we could, and if we did it awkwardly, it should not be set down against us. Had we been called upon to fight for her, we would not have asked about the odds, but would have sailed in, tooth and toe-nail. When we tried to speak to her we just choked up and stood still. We buried Olds that same evening, about sixty feet from the spot where he was killed, just southeast of Rath's store.

The Indians that had caused the alarm numbered between twenty-five and thirty, and were up the valley of Adobe Walls Creek headed east. Finally, they disappeared, and we did not see them again. They may not have belonged to the attacking party, but merely been passing through the country.

I always regretted that I did not keep the relics I picked up at Adobe Walls. Mrs. Olds asked me for the lance when I returned to the building, and I gave it to her. The other relics I took to Dodge City, and gave them away to first one person and then another.

CHAPTER X

THE warriors that attacked Adobe Walls made an extensive raid. Writing from Cheyenne Agency, at Darlington, in September, 1874, a Government employee gave this information to the Commissioner of Indian Affairs:

"We are informed by Little Robe, White Shield, and other Cheyennes that Lone Wolf, a Kiowa chief, was the first to commence the present Indian trouble, by going with a band of his warriors on a raid into Texas. Big Bow, a Comanche, soon followed. After these parties returned, the Kiowas, Comanches, and Cheyennes made the attack upon Adobe Walls. After that fight the combined forces separated into a number of war parties; some went into Texas, others into New Mexico and Colorado, and still others along the Fort Sill and Wichita Railroad and the Kansas border. We have had well-authenticated accounts from Indians and from other sources that the number of individuals killed in New Mexico amounted to 40; Colorado, 60; Lone Wolf's first raid into Texas, 7; Big Bow's first raid into Texas, 4; the Adobe Walls fight, 3; southwest from Camp Supply, buffalo-hunters, 3; between Camp Supply and Dodge, buffalo-hunters, 5; in the vicinity of

184

Medicine Lodge and Sun City, 12; on Crooked Creek, 2; on the trail north from Cheyenne Agency, 5; on the Atchison, Topeka & Santa Fe Railroad, 4; Washita and Fort Sill agencies and vicinity, 14; by Dr. Holloway's son, Cheyenne Agency, 1. Mr. Dougherty, beef contractor for these three agencies reports at least 30 persons recently killed in Texas; total, 190.

"White Shield this day informed me that the Kiowa chief, White Horse, on his last raid into Texas killed eleven persons and captured three children. The children, he states, are now in the Kiowa camps. White Shield says he has heard of several other captives with the Comanches and Kiowas, but these three mentioned are all he has seen."

It has been said that the Indians abandoned the fight because of the wounding of Quanah Parker, the Comanche chief, and again because the "medicine" man found that his "medicine" was bad. To be more exact, the Indians probably came to the conclusion that if they remained long enough, charged often enough and got close enough, all of them would be killed, as they were unable to dislodge us from the buildings.

In the fall of 1877, many of the Comanches became dissatisfied with their life on the military reservation at Fort Sill and fled to their old home on the Staked Plains. Chas. Goodnight was running his cattle in the lower end of Palo Duro, and the Comanches were soon killing beef. When he heard of it, he mounted his horse and rode down to where they were and made a private peace treaty with them, agreeing to give them two beeves a day as long as they remained, if they would not raid his herd. His proposal was accepted, and the compact was kept until the soldiers arrived and compelled the Comanches to return to their reservation.

I met Quanah at that time, having gone out with the troops. As we were riding along one day, he began talking about the fight at the Walls. When I told him that I was one of the men that had fought against him, he leaned over on his horse and shook my hand. We became good friends.

A number of different stories have been related about Quanah's mishaps in the fight. A man who knew him well in later years said that Quanah told him that early in the fight on the first day his horse was shot and killed at a distance of between 400 and 500 yards from the buildings. The horse fell suddenly, pitching Quanah headlong to the ground, his gun falling from his grasp and bounding away. When Quanah saw that his horse was dead, he took shelter behind an old buffalo carcass over which wood-rats had piled weeds and grass, making a heap about waist high. Then something happened that Quanah was never able to explain. He was struck a terrific blow between his shoulder blade and his neck. He was badly stunned but managed to gain his feet and ran and hid himself in a plum thicket. At first he thought somebody had hit him with a heavy stone, but as only his own men could have done this, he abandoned this notion and concluded that he had been hit by a spent or deflected bullet. His right shoulder was useless most of the day, and he could raise his gun with difficulty. He left the battle-ground by riding behind another Indian.

Had it not been for the cracking of the cottonwood ridge pole in Hanrahan's saloon, the Indians would have come upon us unawares and all of us would have been killed, yet we never could find a single thing wrong with the log. Every hunter that came in after the fight, as well as every man at the Walls, examined that cottonwood ridge log over and over to find the break, but it could not be found. The two men who were sleeping in the building declared that the noise sounded like the report of a rifle.

The fight at Adobe Walls broke up buffalo-hunting in that section just as the Indians had planned. This was the last buffalo-hunting I ever did as a business. Hanrahan owned a big outfit and lost everything.

We were now so strong in numbers and so many days had passed without the coming of relief from Dodge that we organized a party of about twenty-five men to go up there and find out why help was not coming. Jim Hanrahan, the oldest man among us, was placed in command. It had now been about a week since the fight.

A serious row was barely averted the night before we pulled out for Dodge. Guns were scarce, and after the death of Olds "Bat" Masterson had borrowed the Olds gun, a better gun than the one used by Masterson, who had lent his gun to another man. When it was learned that we were going to Dodge, Mrs. Olds sent for her husband's gun. "Bat" sent back word that he wanted to keep the gun until morning, promising that he would promptly return it at that time. This was not agreeable to Mrs. Olds, and she sent a man named Brown to Hanrahan's to get the gun without further talk, as she feared that she might lose it.

Brown made a few mistakes in his language in discussing the matter with Hanrahan, the latter having said several times that he would be personally responsible for the gun and would guarantee that it was returned to Mrs. Olds. Brown crowded matters until Hanrahan grabbed him by the nape of the neck and the seat of the trousers, shook him as a bulldog would a kitten, and then threw Brown out of the saloon, saying, "Get out of my building, you———,———— —"! Hanrahan drew his own gun and had Brown covered, ready to pull the trigger, which I believe he would have done, if several of us had not disarmed him, and then reasoned with him not to go any further, because if shooting began there was no telling what might happen, as both men had friends. Next morning "Bat" returned the gun to Mrs. Olds.

The row spread ill feeling among a number of the men, and though blood that had been spilt in fighting for each other was scarcely dry on the ground, yet some were now ready to begin fighting each other. This was the way of the West in those times—every tub had to stand on its own bottom every minute of the day. It was the code that every able-bodied man had to live by. If, however, a man should fall sick or be in bad luck or crippled, the boys stuck to him until he was able to take care of himself. The quarrel caused a little coolness among the men for, as we rode away next morning and were passing Myers & Leonard's store, the men there yelled out, "Goodbye, we don't care for any of you leaving, except Billy Dixon. Three cheers for Billy Dixon!" I waved my hat in acknowledgment of this friendly expression.

We went up Short Creek until we got out on the Plains, where we left the main-traveled freight road and bore more to the west, as we felt that the Indians might be watching this main road. We made it to the head of the Palo Duro the first day and went into camp. By making a long ride our next camp was San Francisco Creek. Here we found where buffalo-hunters had built a camp, and the body of Charley Sharp, who had been killed by the Indians. He had been dead about a week, and the body was shockingly mutilated. Sharp was a partner of Henry Lease, and had remained in camp while Lease went to Adobe Walls for supplies. Sharp bore the nickname "Dublin." Sharp's Creek in Beaver County, Oklahoma, bears his name. We buried the body where we found it.

Bearing to the northeast, we came into the Dodge City and Adobe Walls road at the Cimarron River. Another day's ride brought us to Crooked Creek. We were now out of dangerous country, and reached Dodge City safe and sound.

Ours was the first crowd to reach Dodge City after the fight at Adobe Walls, and the whole town turned out to see us. Everybody was anxious to learn the particulars, and we were asked thousands of questions. News of what had happened at the Walls had driven most of the buffalo-hunters to Dodge City, their camps stretching up and down the Arkansas near town.

We learned that a relief party, composed of buffalo-hunters and residents of Dodge, had started south under the command of Tom Nixon. There were about forty men in the party. Nixon was killed nearly ten years later by "Mysterious Dave" Matthews. He was a well-known frontiersman.

We did not take life nor ourselves very seriously those days, and were soon entering into the fun at Dodge with the greatest enthusiasm, forgetful of the perils and hardships that so lately beset us. Things at Dodge were run for the fullest enjoyment of the present. There was not much material to occupy students of ancient history. The town had changed little since we had gone away. Several of the men who had come north from the Walls went straight to the depot and bought tickets for their homes in the east. They had had enough of the Indians to last them several years, and were not ashamed to stand up and say so. Most of us were "locoed" with the work and the sport of the land where the wool was long and the customs wild. Drouth, scarcity of water-holes, northers, rattlesnakes, Indians, even the United States Army could not have driven us east of the ninety-ninth meredian. We were hardened to danger and rather enjoyed adventure. Soon everything would be quiet again and life would go on in the same old way. We were determined to stay with the game.

The details of the fight at Adobe Walls were telegraphed to Fort Leavenworth. Troops were not despatched at once to the scene of the uprising, the Government taking the view that it would be best not to move until an expedition large enough to whip the Indians to a standstill could be sent into the field. General Miles reached Dodge City about the first of August, going south about a week later.

My old friend Jack Callahan, of whom I have frequently spoken, had just been employed as wagonmaster to go with the expedition. Meeting me in the street, he offered to make me his assistant. I had made up my mind to accept the position, but further down the street I came across John Curley, whom I had known at Hays City in 1868, when he was corral-master. Curley said that he believed he could get me placed as scout and guide with General Miles, which exactly suited me. We went at once to General Miles' headquarters, where Curley introduced and recommended me. After asking me a few questions, General Miles turned to his adjutant and told him to put my name down. I held this position from August 6, 1874, to February 10, 1883.

The troops moved out of Dodge City to the Arkansas and camped. General Miles assembled his scouts and tested their marksmanship by having them shoot at snags in the river, calling our names as he pointed out the objects each was to shoot at. I never missed a single time.

Lieutenant Frank D. Baldwin, now a brigadier-general, was sent to Adobe Walls with two scouts, six Delaware trailers and a troop of cavalry to ascertain the situation of those who had remained at the Walls. Baldwin had not recently seen much mounted service, and was very tired and saddle-worn by the time we reached Adobe Walls Creek.

About 4 o'clock in the afternoon of the day as we neared the Walls, Baldwin seeing that night would come before we arrived, ordered "Bat" Masterson and myself to ride ahead and tell the boys that the troops were coming. This precaution was taken lest the buffalo-hunters might mistake us for Indians and fire into us. I rode up within speaking distance and hallooed to the men and waved my hat, to let them know who I was. Recognizing me, they gave me a hearty reception. There were a dozen or more men in the buildings, where they had been shut up for more than a month. At no time had they ventured far away. They had kept their horses in the stockade, fearful of an attack by Indians; hay for the horses had been cut in the creek bottom. When Tom Nixon and his men came down from Dodge, Mrs. Olds and the greater part of the men went back with him. A number, however, preferred to remain at the Walls, however great the risk, and did so. The boys cooked me a hot supper and I was telling them stories of the outside world when the soldiers arrived about 9 o'clock.

The water in Adobe Walls Creek was now so low that there was not enough for the horses; so we pulled over on Bent's Creek, and camped on a mesquite flat, just north of the old Adobe Walls ruins.

Next morning Lieutenant Baldwin asked me to walk over the battleground with him. Practically all the men went with us, the distance being about a mile. The coming of the soldiers had given a feeling of security to the men at the Walls, who now turned out their horses to graze. Everybody was laughing and talking and telling jokes, without the slightest thought of danger. Some mischievous fellow had stuck an Indian's skull on each post of the corral gate.

Tobe Robinson and George Huffman, civilians, rode down the valley toward the Canadian River to hunt wild plums which at that time were ripe and plentiful. They had been gone only a short

time when our attention was drawn to two horse-
men riding at top speed from the direction of the
river toward the Walls. Behind them came ten
or fifteen Indians quirting their ponies at every
jump. The two men were Robinson and Huffman. They had unexpectedly run into a band
of Indians who were doing their best to circle and
cut off the two white men. There we stood a mile
from camp where our arms lay, unable to render
these men any assistance in their desperate straits.

Robinson and Huffman were riding side by side
and were able to maintain this position until they
were rounding a little knoll just beyond the old
ruins. Here an Indian managed to ride up near
enough to run his lance through Huffman's body.
Huffman fell dead from his horse.

The riderless horse continued running beside
Robinson's, the Indian still pursuing, grabbing
again and again at the rein of Huffman's horse.
Finally, he seized the rein, checked the horse, and
rode back at full speed toward his companions. All
the Indians now galloped away and disappeared
among the sand hills.

The tragedy had happened so quickly that we
could hardly believe our eyes. The Indians made
no effort to mutilate or carry off Huffman's body.
Robinson reached us in safety, though shaking
with excitement. From the Indian standpoint,
the warrior who had killed Huffman and escaped
with his horse had covered himself with glory.

Sight of the tents in the mesquite flat doubtless caused the other Indians to give up the chase, or else both Huffman and Robinson would have been lanced to death.

Considerable time was lost in rounding up our horses, which were grazing in the valley, and getting into our saddles before we got on the trail of the Indians. Before we could reach the Canadian the Indians had vanished in the sandhills of White Deer Creek. We found two fagged ponies that the Indians had abandoned.

We carried Huffman's body to the Walls and dug a grave close beside the other graves. This made five graves. Some day I hope a stone will be erected to mark the spot. These men gave all they had—their lives—to help make this a civilized country.

Next day the soldiers and the men we found at the Walls started south to join the main command on Cantonment Creek. We crossed the Canadian near the mouth of Tallahone, where J. A. King now has a cow ranch. On Chicken Creek we found two Indians who had stopped for noon, and had built a small fire. Their ponies were near at hand, tied to some sagebrush, and their blankets had been spread out on the ground to dry. We succeeded in killing one of them, but the other warrior certainly had a fine quality of stuff in his "medicine" bag, for he mounted his pony and got away, despite the bullets that split the air around him. He was too hard-pressed to get his blanket and a butcher knife which he left sticking in the ground.

The noise of our guns stampeded a big bunch of buffalo further up the creek. They kicked up such a cloud of dust that we thought a war party of Indians, possibly the same that had attacked Adobe Walls, was coming for us, and that we had stirred up the worst kind of trouble. Happily, we were soon able to see the buffalo, and the world looked brighter.

"Old Nigger" Clark, our cook, driving a six-mule team, with bedding, provisions and cooking outfit, was a long way behind when the shooting began. He raised a welt every time he hit a mule, and by the time he drew near us he was making the fastest kind of time, his eyes sticking out like saucers. When almost upon us, his mules took fright and ran away, and could not be stopped until men rode to his assistance.

Ours was the last party of white men to leave Adobe Walls. When I passed that way the following fall with United States troops the Indians had been there and burned the place to the ground. The walls were still smoking.

General Miles was with us on this trip. We camped in sight of the battleground. He asked hundreds of questions about the fight, appearing curious about every detail. The soldiers picked up everything they could find in their hunt for souvenirs, even bones, which I am sure were mostly horse bones. The Indians had gathered up all the bones of their dead and wrapped them in new blankets, depositing them at the foot of the hills on the east side of the valley of Adobe Walls Creek. The soldiers threw away the bones and carried off the blankets. This was in October. The Indians had not taken any of the provisions which had been left in the buildings. They were a suspicious people, and were fearful that the provisions might be poisoned.

While we were at Adobe Walls on this last trip, a dog that I had owned at the time of the fight came into camp. Her appearance affected me greatly, as I was fond of her; in fact, I have always had an affection for dumb animals. She was a highly intelligent setter bitch, named Fannie. She had disappeared with the other dogs the day of the fight, and I was sure that she had been killed by the Indians or had wandered away and starved. Several months had passed since I had seen her.

After we had petted her and fed her, Fannie disappeared. But her absence was brief. She came back with something in her mouth and stood wagging her tail, to attract attention. When we saw what she had brought to us every man grinned and was as tickled as if he were a boy. Fannie had brought a fat, bright-eyed little puppy in her mouth. Dropping the little fellow gently on a pile of bedding, she frisked about with delight as each of us tried to get hold of the pup and fondle it. Fannie bounded away while we were "fussing" among ourselves to see who should play with the pup. She came with another pup in her mouth, leaving it beside the other one. She made two more trips, until finally her family of four little ones were playing with each other on our bedding. The father of these pups was the big Newfoundland that belonged to the Shadler brothers, which the Indians killed while he was trying to defend his masters at the very beginning of the Adobe Walls fight. When we pulled out, Fannie and her babies were given a snug place in the mess wagon.

CHAPTER XI

THE most perilious adventure of my life occurred September 12, 1874, in what was known as the Buffalo Wallow Fight. My escape from death was miraculous. The year 1874, as the reader doubtless may have observed, brought me full measure of things I had dreamed of doing when a boy. I came in contact with hostile Indians as frequently as the most devoted warrior might wish, and found that fighting them was serious business.

On September 10, 1874, General Nelson A. Miles, in command of the troops campaigning against the Indians in the Southwest, was on McClellan Creek, in the Panhandle, when he ordered Amos Chapman and myself, scouts, and four enlisted men to carry dispatches to Fort Supply. The enlisted men were Sergeant Z. T. Woodhull, Troop I; Private Peter Rath, Troop A; Private John Harrington, Troop H; and Private George W. Smith, Troop M, Sixth Cavalry. When General Miles handed us the dispatches, he told us that we could have all the soldiers we thought necessary. His command was short of rations. We preferred the smallest possible number.

For most of the first two nights out from camp we

199

traveled, resting in secluded places during the day. War parties were moving in every direction, and there was danger of attack at every turn. On the second day, just as the sun was rising, we were nearing a divide between the Washita River and Gageby Creek. Riding to the top of a little knoll, we found ourselves almost face to face with a large band of Kiowa and Comanche warriors. The Indians saw us at the same instant and, circling quickly, surrounded us. We were in a trap. We knew that the best thing to do was to make a stand and fight for our lives, as there would be great danger of our becoming separated in the excitement of a running fight, after which the Indians could the more easily kill us one by one. We also realized that we could do better work on foot; so we dismounted and placed our horses in the care of George Smith. In a moment or two poor Smith was shot down, and the horses stampeded.

When Smith was shot, he felt flat on his stomach, and his gun fell from his hand, far beyond his reach. But no Indian was ever able to capture that gun; if one ventured near Smith, we never failed to bring him down. We thought Smith was dead when he fell, but he survived until about 11 o'clock that night.

I realized at once that I was in closer quarters than I had ever been in in my life, and I have always felt that I did some good work that day. I was fortunate enough not to become disabled at any stage of the fight, which left me free to do my best

under the circumstances. I received one wound—
a bullet in the calf of my leg. I was wearing a
thin cashmere shirt, slightly bloused. This shirt
was literally riddled with bullets. How a man
could be shot at so many times at close range and
not be hit I could never understand. The Indians
seemed to feel absolutely sure of getting us, so
sure, in fact, that they delayed riding us down and
killing us at once, which they could easily have
done, and prolonged the early stages of the fight
merely to satisfy their desire to toy with an enemy
at bay, as a cat would play with a mouse before
taking its life.

We saw that there was no show for us to survive
on this little hillside, and decided that our best
fighting ground was a small mesquite flat several
hundred yards distant. Before we undertook to
shift our position a bullet struck Amos Chapman.
I was looking at him when he was shot. Amos
said, "Billy, I am hit at last," and eased himself
down. The fight was so hot that I did not have
time to ask him how badly he was hurt. Every
man, save Rath and myself, had been wounded.
Our situation was growing more desperate every
minute. I knew that something had to be done,
and quickly, or else all of us in a short while
would be dead or in the hands of the Indians, who
would torture as in the most inhuman manner
before taking our lives.

I could see where the buffalo had pawed and
wallowed a depression commonly called a buffalo

"wallow," and I ran for it at top speed. It seemed as if a bullet whizzed past me at every jump, but I got through unharmed. The wallow was about ten feet in diameter. I found that its depth, though slight, afforded some protection. I shouted to my comrades to try to come to me, which all of them save Smith and Chapman, commenced trying to do. As each man reached the wallow, he drew his butcher knife and began digging desperately with knife and hands to throw up the dirt round the sides. The land happened to be sandy, and we made good headway, though constantly interrupted by the necessity of firing at the Indians as they dashed within range.

It was probably about noon before we reached the wallow. Many times that terrible day did I think that my last moment was at hand. Once, when the Indians were crowding us awfully hard, one of the boys raised up and yelled, "No use, boys, no use; we might as well give it up." We answered by shouting to him to lie down. At that moment a bullet struck in the soft bank near him and completely filled his mouth with dirt. I was so amused that I laughed, though in a rather sickly way, for none of us felt much like laughing.

By this time, however, I had recovered from the first excitement of battle, and was perfectly cool, as were the rest of the men. We were keenly aware that the only thing to do was to sell our lives as dearly as possible. We fired deliberately, taking good aim, and were picking off an Indian at almost

Ermoke and His Band of Murderous Kiowa Raiders

every round. The wounded men conducted themselves admirably, and greatly assisted in concealing our crippled condition by sitting upright, as if unhurt, after they reached the wallow. This made it impossible for the Indians accurately to guess what plight we were in. Had they known so many of us were wounded undoubtedly they would have ridden in and finished us.

After all had reached the wallow, with the exception of Chapman and Smith, all of us thinking that Smith was dead, somebody called to Chapman to come on it. We now learned for the first time that Chapman's leg was broken. He called back that he could not walk, as his left knee was shattered.

I made several efforts to reach him before I succeeded. Every time the Indians saw me start, they would fire such a volley that I was forced to retreat, until finally I made a run and got to Chapman. I told him to climb on my back, my plan being to carry him as I would a little child. Drawing both his legs in front of me in such a way as to support the broken one over the sound one, I carried him to the wallow, though not without difficulty, as he was a larger man than myself and his body was a dead weight. It taxed my strength to carry him.

We were now all in the wallow, except Smith, and we felt that it would be foolish and useless to risk our lives in attempting to bring in his dead body. We had not seen him move since the moment he went down. We began digging like gophers with our hands and knives to make our little wall of earth higher, and shortly had heaped up quite a little wall of dirt around us. Its protection was quickly felt, even though our danger was hardly lessened.

When I look back and recall our situation, I always find myself thinking of how my wounded companions never complained nor faltered, but fought as bravely as if not a bullet had touched them. Sometimes the Indians would ride toward us at headlong speed with lances uplifted and poised, undoubtedly bent upon spearing us. Such moments made a man brace himself and grip his gun. Fortunately, we were able to keep our heads and to bring down or disable the leader. Such charges proved highly dangerous to the Indians, and gradually grew less frequent.

Thus, all that long, hot September day the Indians circled round us or dashed past, yelling and cutting all kinds of capers. All morning we had been without water, and the wounded were sorely in need of it. In the stress and excitement of such an encounter, even a man who has not been hurt grows painfully thirsty, and his tongue and lips are soon as dry as a whetstone. Ours was the courage of despair. We knew what would befall us if we should be captured alive—we had seen too many naked and mangled bodies of white men who had been spread-eagled and tortured with steel and fire to forget what our own fate would be. So we were determined to fight to the end, not unmindful of the fact that every once in a while there was another dead or wounded Indian.

About 3 o'clock a black cloud came up in the west, and in a short time the sky shook and blazed with thunder and lightning. Rain fell in blinding sheets, drenching us to the skin. Water gathered quickly in the buffalo wallow, and our wounded men eagerly bent forward and drank from the muddy pool. It was more than muddy—that water was red with their own blood that had flowed from their wounds and lay clotting and dry in the hot September sun.

The storm and the rain proved our salvation. The wind had shifted to the north and was now chilling us to the bone. An Indian dislikes rain, especially a cold rain, and these Kiowas and Comanches were no exception to the rule. We could see them in groups out of rifle range sitting on their horses with their blankets drawn tightly around them. The Plains country beats the world for quick changes in weather, and in less than an hour after the rain had fallen, the wind was bitterly cold. Not a man in our crowd had a coat, and our thin shirts were scant protection. Our coats were tied behind our saddles when our horses stampeded, and were lost beyond recovery. I was heart-sick over the loss of my coat, for in the inside pocket was my dearest treasure, my mother's picture, which my father had given me shortly before his death. I was never able to recover it.

The water was gathering rapidly in the wallow and soon had reached a depth of two inches. Not a man murmured. Not one thought of surrender. The wounded were shivering as if they had ague.

We now found that our ammunition was running low. This fact rather appalled us, as bullets, and plenty of them, were our only protection. At the fight at the Walls, not only was there plenty of ammunition, but the buildings themselves gave confidence. Necessity compelled us to save every cartridge as long as possible, and not to fire at an Indian unless we could see that he meant business and was coming right into us.

Late in the afternoon somebody suggested that we go out and get Smith's belt and six-shooter, as he had been shot early in the fight and his belt undoubtedly was loaded with cartridges.

Rath offered to go, and soon returned with word that Smith was still alive. The news astonished us, and the fact that we had neglected him, even though in ignorance, filled us with regret. Rath and I at once got ready to bring Smith to the buffalo wallow. By supporting himself between us, he managed to walk. We could see that there was no chance for him. He was shot through the left lung and when he breathed the wind sobbed out of his back under the shoulder blade. Near the wallow an Indian had dropped a

stout willow switch with which he had been whipping his pony. With this switch a silk handker-
chief was stuffed into the gaping bullet hole in
Smith's back.

Night was approaching, and it looked blacker
to me than any night I had ever seen. Ours was
a forlorn and disheartening situation. The Indians were still all around us. The nearest relief
was seventy-five miles away. Of the six men in
the wallow, four were badly wounded, and without anything to relieve their suffering. We were
cold and hungry, with nothing to eat, and without
a blanket, coat or hat to protect us from the rain
and the biting wind. It was impossible to rest
or sleep in the water in the wallow.

I remember that I threw my hat, a wide-
brimmed sombrero, as far from me as I could
when our horses stampeded—the hat was in my
way and too good a target for the Indians to
shoot at.

We were unable to get grass for bedding, as the
whole country had been burnt off by the Indians.
It was absolutely necessary, however, that the men
should have some kind of bed to keep them off the
cold, damp ground. Rath and I solved the problem by gathering tumble-weeds, which in that
country the wind would drive for miles and miles
until they lodged and became fast. Many of them
were bigger than a bushel basket, and their twigs
were so tough that the weeds had the "spring"
of a wire matress. We crushed the weeds and

lay down on them for the night, though not a man dared close his eyes in sleep.

By the time heavy darkness had fallen every Indian had disappeared. Happily, they did not return to molest us during the night. There was a new moon, but so small and slender that in the clouded sky there was little light. While there was still light, I took the willow switch and sat down on the edge of the bank and carefully cleaned every gun.

While I was cleaning the guns, we held a consultation to decide what would be best for us to do. We agreed that somebody should go for help. No journey could have been beset with greater danger. Rath and I both offered to go. The task was squarely up to us, as all the other men were injured. I insisted that I should go, as I knew the country, and felt confident that I could find the trail that led to Camp Supply. I was sure that we were not far from this trail.

My insistence at once caused protest from the wounded. They were willing that Rath should go, but would not listen to my leaving them. Once I put my hand on my gun with the intention of going anyway, then yielded to their wishes against my better judgment, and decided to remain through the night. The wounded men relied greatly upon my skill as a marksman.

Bidding us goodbye, Rath disappeared in the darkness. After he had been gone about two hours he came back, saying that he could not find the trail.

By this time Smith had grown much worse and was begging us in piteous tones to shoot him and put an end to his terrible sufferings. We found it necessary to watch him closely to prevent him from taking his own life.

There was not a man among us who had not thought of that same melancholy fate. When the fight was at its worst, with the Indians closing in on all sides, and when it seemed that every minute would be our last, I was strongly tempted to take my butcher knife, which I kept at razor edge, and cut off my hair. In those days my hair was black and heavy and brushed my shoulders. As a matter of fact, I was rather proud of my hair. Its luxuriance would have tempted any Indian to scalp me at the first opportunity. I had a further and final plan—to save my last bullet for self-destruction.

Poor Smith endured his agony like a brave soldier. Our hearts ached but we could do nothing to relieve his pain. About 10 o'clock that night he fell asleep and we were glad of it, for in sleep he could forget his sufferings. Later in the night one of the boys felt of him, to see how he was getting along. He was cold in death. Men commonly think of death as something to be shunned. There are times, however, when its hand falls as tenderly as the touch of a mother's hand, and when

its coming is welcomed by those to whom hopeless
sufferings has brought the last bitter dregs of life.
We lifted the body of our dead comrade and gently
laid it outside the buffalo wallow on the mesquite
grass, covering the white face with a silk handker-
chief.

Then the rest of us huddled together on the damp
ground, and thought of the morrow. That night is
indelibly stamped in my memory; many a time
have its perils filled my dreams, until I awoke
startled and thrilled by a feeling of imminent
danger. Every night the same stars are shining
way out there in the Panhandle, the winds sigh
as mournfully as they did then, and I often wonder
if a single settler who passes the lonely spot knows
how desperately six men once battled for their lives
where now may be plowed fields and safety and
the comforts of civilization.

Like everything else, the long night finally
came to an end, and the sum rose clear and warm
next morning. By this time all the men were
willing that I should go for help, and I at once
started. Daylight exposed me to many dangers
from which the night shielded me. By moving
cautiously at night, it was possible to avoid the
enemy, but if surprised, to stand a good chance of
escape. In the daytime, however, the enemy could
lie in hiding and scan the country in every direction. On the Plains, especially in the fall when
the grass is brown, the smallest moving object may
be perceived by the trained eye at an astonishingly

long distance. I knew that I must proceed with utmost caution, lest I fall into an ambush or be attacked in the open by superior numbers.

I had traveled scarcely more than half a mile when I struck the plain trail leading to Camp Supply. Hurrying along as rapidly as possible and keeping a constant lookout for Indians, I checked myself at the sudden sight of an outfit that seemed to cover about an acre of ground, two miles or so to the northwest. The outfit at first did not appear to be moving and I could not tell whether it was made up of white men or Indians. I skulked to a growth of tall grass and hid for a while. My nerves were too keen to endure hiding and waiting, so I stole back and took another look. The outfit was moving toward me. Shortly I was able to see that they were troops; Indians always traveled strung out in a line, while these were traveling abreast.

I never felt happier in my life. I whanged loose with my rifle to attract the attention of the soldiers, and saw the whole command come to a halt. I fired my gun a second time, which brought two soldiers to me. I told them of our condition, and they rode rapidly back to the command and reported. The commanding officer was Major William R. Price of the 8th U. S. Cavalry with a troop accompanying General Miles' supply train, which was on its way with supplies from Fort Supply to field headquarters.

The same Indians that we had been fighting

had been holding this supply train, which, under the escort of a detachment commanded by Capt. Wyllys Lyman, 5th U. S. Infantry, had been corralled for four days near the Washita River. Major Price, luckily for the outfit, happened along and raised the siege. The Indians had just given up the attack when we ran into them.

Major Price rode over to where I was waiting, bringing his army surgeon with him. I described the condition of my comrades, after which Major Price sent the surgeon and two soldiers to see what could be done for the wounded. I pointed out the place, which was about a mile distant, and asked the surgeon if he thought he could find it without my going along, as Major Price wanted me to tell him about the fight. The surgeon said that he could and rode away.

I was describing in detail all that had happened when I looked up and saw that the relief party was bearing too far north. I fired my gun to attract their attention, and then waved it in the direction which they were to go. By this time they were within gunshot of my comrades in the buffalo wallow. To my utter astonishment, I heard the roar of a gun and saw a puff of smoke rise from the wallow. One of the men had fired at the approaching strangers, killing a horse ridden by one of the soldiers.

I ran forward as rapidly as possible, not knowing what the men would do next. They were soon able to recognize me, and lowered their guns.

When we got to them the men said that they had heard shooting—the shots I had fired to attract the attention of the troops—and supposed that the Indians had killed me and were coming for them. They were determined to take no chances, and shot at the surgeon and the two soldiers the moment they got within range.

Despite the sad plight of the wounded men, about all the surgeons did was to examine their injuries. The soldiers turned over a few pieces of hardtack and some dried beef, which happened to be tied behind their saddles. Major Price refused to leave any men with us. For this he was afterwards severely censured, and justly. He would not even provide us with firearms. Our own ammunition was exhausted and the soldiers carried guns of different make and caliber from ours. However, they said they would let General Miles know of our condition. We were sure that help would come the moment General Miles heard the news. At the time we were glad just to have seen these men and did not think much about how they treated us.

We watched and waited until midnight of the second day after the troops had passed before help came. A long way off in the dark we heard the faint sound of a bugle. It made us swallow a big lump in our throats and bite our lips. Nearer and clearer came the bugle notes. Our nerves were getting "jumpy," so strong was our emotion. We fired our guns, to let them know where we were, and soon the soldiers came riding out of the darkness.

As soon as the wounded could be turned over to the surgeon, we placed the body of our dead comrade in the wallow where we had all fought and suffered together, and covered it with the dirt which we had ridged up with our hands and butcher knives for breastworks. Then we went down on the creek, where the soldiers built a big fire and cooked a meal for us.

Next day the wounded were sent to Camp Supply, where they were given humane and careful treatment. Amos Chapman's leg was amputated above the knee. Amos was as tough as second growth hickory and was soon out of the hospital and in the saddle. All the men recovered and went right on with the army. Chapman could handle a gun and ride as well as ever, the only difference being that he had to mount his horse from the right side, Indian fashion.

I should like once more to meet the men with whom I fought in the Buffalo Wallow Fight, but I seldom hear from them. When I last heard of Amos Chapman he was living at Seiling, Oklahoma.[1] My last letter from Sergeant Woodhall was dated Fort· Wingate, New Mexico, 1883. This was shortly after Colonel Dodge had published his book, *Our Wild Indians,* in which he attempted to give a circumstantial account of the Buffalo Wallow Fight. Sergeant Woodhall was

[1] He died the latter part of 1925

displeased with the statement of facts, and resented the inaccuracies.

I guess I am partly to blame in the matter. When Colonel Dodge was writing his book, he wrote and asked me to send him an account of the fight. I neglected to do so, and he obtained his information from other sources. If my present narrative differs from that of Colonel Dodge, all I can say is that I have described the fight as I saw it. In saying this I do not wish to place myself in the attitude of censuring Colonel Dodge. However, it should be reasonably apparent that a man with a broken leg cannot carry another man on his back. In correcting this bit of border history I repeat that every one of my comrades in that fight conducted himself in the most heroic manner, bravely doing his part in every emergency. Below will be found the text of the report which General Miles sent to Washington:

Headquarters Indian Territory Expedition,
    Camp on Washita River, Texas,
        September 24, 1874.

Adjutant General, U. S. A.,
    Thro Offices Asst. Adjt. Gen., Headquarters Department and Military Division of the Missouri and of the Army.

General:

I deem it but a duty to brave men and faithful soldiers to bring to the notice of the highest military authority, an instance of indomitable courage, skill and true heroism on the part of a detachment from this command, with the request that the actors may be rewarded, and their faithfulness and bravery recognized, by pensions, medals of honor, or in such way as may be deemed most fitting. On the night of the 10th inst. a party consisting of Sergt. Z. T. Woodhall, Co. I; Privates Peter Rath, Co. A; John Harrington, Co. H., and George W. Smith, Co. M., Sixth Cavalry; Scouts Amos Chapman and William Dixon, were sent as bearers of despatches from the camp of this command on McClellan Creek to Camp Supply, I. T.

At 6 a. m., of the 12th, when approaching the Washita River, they were met and surrounded by a band of Kiowa and Comanches, who had scarcely left their Agency; at the first attack all were struck, Private Smith mortally, and three others severely wounded. Although enclosed on all sides and by overwhelming numbers, one of them succeeded, while they were under a heavy fire at short range, and while the others, with their rifles, were keeping the Indians at bay, in digging with his knife and hands a slight cover. After this had been secured, they placed themselves within it, the wounded walking with brave and painful efforts, and Private Smith, though he had received a mortal wound, sitting upright within the trench, to conceal the crippled condition of their party from the Indians,

From early morning till dark, outnumbered 25 to 1, under an almost constant fire and at such short range that they sometimes used their pistols, retaining the last charge to prevent capture and torture, this little party of five defended their lives and the person of their dying comrade, without food, and their only drink the rain water that collected in a pool mingled with their own blood.

There is no doubt but that they killed more than double their number, besides those that were wounded. The Indians abandoned the attack on the 12th at dark.

The exposure and distance from the command, which were necessary incidents of their duty, were such, that for thirty-six hours from the first attack, their condition could not be known, and not till midnight of the 13th could they receive medical attendance and food, exposed during this time to an incessant cold storm.

Sergt. Woodhall, Private Harrington and Scout Chapman were seriously wounded. Private Smith died of his wounds on the morning of the 13th. Private Rath and Scout Dixon were struck but not disabled.

The simple recital of their deeds, and the mention of the odds against which they fought, how the wounded defended the dying, and the dying aided the wounded by exposure to fresh wounds after the power of action was gone, these alone present a scene of cool courage, heroism and self-

218 LIFE OF "BILLY" DIXON

sacrifice which duty, as well as inclination prompts us to recognize, but which we cannot fully honor.

Very Respectfully,
Your obedient servant,
(Signed)   NELSON A. MILES,
Col. and Bvt. Maj. Gen'l. U. S. A., Commanding.

Headquarters Indian Territory Expedition, Camp on Oasis Creek, I. T.,
Oct. 1, 1874.

Official copy respectfully furnished William Dixon. By command of Bvt. Maj. Gen'l. Miles.

G. W. BAIRD,
Asst. Adjt. 5th Inf., A. A. A. Gen'l.

General Miles had both the heart and the accomplishments of a soldier, and Congress voted to each of us the Medal of Honor. He was delighted when the Medals came from Washington. With his own hands he pinned mine on my coat when we were in camp on Carson Creek, five or six miles west of the ruins of the original Adobe Walls. The text of the official correspondence concerning the award of the Medals of Honor is appended:

Headquarters Indian Territory Expedition, Camp near Fort Sill, I. T.,
January 24th, 1875.

General Order No. 28:

The Commanding Officer takes pleasure in announcing to the troops of this Expedition that his recommendation that the distinguished heroism displayed on the 12th of September, 1874 by Sergeant Z. T. Woodhall of Co. I, Private John Harrington, Co. H, and Peter Rath Co. A, 6th Cavalry, and Scouts Amos Chapman and William Dixon be recognized, has been approved by the highest military authority, and that the Congress has bestowed upon each of these men a Medal of Honor. It is now his pleasing duty to bestow upon men who can worthily wear them, these tokens of the recognition and approval of their Government.

By Command of Bvt. Maj. Gen'l. N. A. Miles.
   (Signed)   G. W. BAIRD,
      1st Lieut. and Adjutant 5th Infty.,
                  A. A. A. General.

Headquarters Ind. Ter. Expedition.
    Camp on Canadian, Texas.
       December 24, 1874.

Mr. William Dixon.

Sir:

I take pleasure in presenting to you a Medal of Honor, as a recognition by the Government of your skill, courage and determined fortitude, displayed in an engagement with (5) others, on the 12th of September, 1874, against hostile Indians, in overwhelming numbers.

This mark of honor, I trust, will be long worn by you, and though it in a small degree compensates for the hardships endured, yet it is a lasting emblem of distinguished services, well earned in a noble cause. It will ever recall the fact to you and yours, of having materially aided in clearing this fair country of ruthless savages, and freeing it from all time to civil settlements. This must be an ever increasing gratification to you.

This badge of honor is most worthily bestowed.

Respectfully, &c.,

NELSON A. MILES,

Bvt. Maj. Gen'l. U. S. Army,

Commanding.

It was always my intention to go back and mark the spot where the Buffalo Wallow Fight took place and where George Smith still lies buried. Procrastination and the remoteness of the spot have prevented my going.

CHAPTER XII

IN civilized surroundings a Plains blizzard is bad
enough; in a wild country, a blizzard is more
appalling than a tornado, for the latter may be
dodged, but the blizzard is everywhere and sets its
teeth into a man's vitals, wherever he may be. A
blizzard brings a feeling of terror that even the
strongest man can hardly resist. I have seen men
moaning and trembling in a blizzard, as if the last
drop of courage had oozed from their bodies.
They were not cowards. Their distress was due
to an instinctive, animal-like feeling that death
was everywhere about them, invisible, dread and
mysterious. In time, however, this fearfulness
wears away, but not until death itself has begun
fastening upon the freezing body. As by drowning, death by freezing is comparatively painless.
In their last hours, natural death usually is kind
to all creatures.

In going from the Canadian River to Camp
Supply, March 17, 1875, with a company of
soldiers, I met with an experience in a blizzard
that I never forgot. The snow had drifted so
deep that the horses soon grew exhausted. My
own horse was badly jaded. The men were suffering with the cold so intensely that they were un-

ruly and hard to control. It was my duty to keep the lead. I was sure that I was going in the right direction, though it was impossible to see more than ten steps ahead.

Occasionally, one of the men would ride ahead of me, contrary to orders, and finally I told the lieutenant who was in command that the men would have to keep back or we would lose our way. He ordered them to stay behind. My horse became so fatigued that he began staggering, and I knew that it was no longer safe to ride him, as he could not be trusted to hold his course, so I dismounted and led him. A soldier, compelled to remain in his saddle, said that he was afraid he was freezing, and asked me to mount his horse that he might have an excuse for walking. I then turned my horse loose.

Pretty soon we came to the forks of a draw. I took the one that I thought led to camp and, luckily, was right. Had we turned up the other prong we would have frozen to death. We had gone only a short distance from the forking when I noticed that the soldier on foot was not in sight. I asked the lieutenant if it might not be well to go back and look for the straggler.

The lieutenant merely shook his head and motioned for me to keep going. His manner displeased me, until I learned that he was so cold that he could not open his mouth—his jaws were set and practically locked.

After riding a few miles, we struck camp.

There was plenty of timber, and we soon had a roaring fire, and thawed out. The soldier on foot was not with us. Three or four of us went back to where the draw pronged, and by the light of a lantern could plainly see his tracks in the snow, and where he had taken the wrong route, going off down the east prong, instead of following us.

We hunted and hunted for him, but could not find him. To our amazement, he came into camp next morning, more dead than alive. His feet were frozen and had to be amputated.

Panhandle weather in the very early spring is the most unreliable in the world. We crawled into our blankets that night, numb and shivering, the wind howling in the timber, and the snow drifting and drifting around our tents. How about next morning? Well, the sun came up next morning, smiling and warm; a soft wind was whispering from the south, and by noon the hills were running with water from the melted snow. When the snow melted from the wild plum bushes we saw that they were in full bloom, and there was not a prettier sight in the Panhandle. There were worlds of plums that year. In two weeks the grass was green everywhere on the Plains, and spring came with a rush.

Once when we were scouting between Wolf Creek and the Canadian River, in the fall of 1875, and were crowding a band of Cheyenne Indians very closely, we ran across an old Indian squaw who had been deserted and left behind by her tribe. She was old and feeble and almost blind. All she had to eat was some wild grapes, which grew plentifully along the creek.

At first she refused to talk and acted in a sullen manner. We gave her a saddle pony and took her along. When we camped for the night some of the soldiers built her a fire off to one side of the main camp, some of them joking with her. But she evidently resented all offers of friendship and at the end of the fourth day while we were camped at noon the old squaw silently rode away. We never knew what became of her.

All old-timers in the southwest remember Jack Stilwell, scout, guide and good fellow. One of his exploits was to escape at night from the island where Major Forsyth, in the battle of the Arickaree, was surrounded by Indians, and go to Fort Wallace for relief. Once Jack and I were out on the Staked Plains with nothing to eat. Jack persuaded me to kill a wild horse for meat. A large herd was grazing at the edge of a lake, and I shot a two-year-old filly. We built a fire and cooked some of the meat. Doing my level best, I was never able to swallow a single mouthful—always it struck in my throat. I preferred to go hungry rather than try to eat it. The meat looked good, but the name was too much for me.

Stilwell was a frolicsome fellow and played many pranks. One time we were going from Camp Supply to Dodge City. Just to make fun on the trip, Jack told me that when we stopped for dinner he would dare me to shoot at his ears, to see what the army officers would do. Noon came and while the officer in charge was looking in our direction, Jack said:

"Billy, I'll bet you can't hit my ear with your rifle."

"All right," I answered, "stand out there where you will not be in the way of the other gentlemen, and I'll see what I can do."

The old army officer looked at us with disgust and later with horror. I was a crack shot, and Jack knew he was safe. Taking careful aim, I fired just as close to his ear as I dared with safety. Jack dodged and scratched his ear as if a hornet had stung him.

"You come pretty close. Try again," he said.

I shot a second time, and Jack repeated his scratching performance, declaring that he was sure I barely missed breaking the skin.

The old army officer scowled at us as if we were devils. He told the men at the next station that we were the toughest bunch he was ever with, and that we had been shooting at each other all day. When the corral master wanted the old officer to ride the rest of the way with us, he positively and emphatically, even profanely refused, saying that we were the wrong kind of roosters for him to be with.

The rescue of the four Germaine sisters who had been captured by the Indians was a romantic incident of the Miles expedition to subdue the hostile tribes in 1875. The circumstances surrounding their capture by the Indians shocked the whole country and inflamed the border settlements with a spirit of vengeance that would have wrought the destruction of every Indian west of the Mississippi had it been possible to attack the marauders at close quarters. From time to time news came from the Indian country that the girls were still alive, and mothers everywhere were praying for the restoration of the captives to their friends.

The fate of the Germaine family was not unlike that of others in those troublous times. John Germaine was a poverty-stricken farmer at Blue Ridge, Fannin County, Georgia, when he returned from service in the Confederate Army in the Civil War. Contending armies had pillaged and devasted his neighborhood. Germaine decided that he would recruit his broken fortune by moving west. With a yoke of oxen and his wife and children, he set out in April, 1870, halting for a time in central Tennessee, where he remained until the following September. Southern Missouri invited him further westward, and he moved to that state, where he took a homestead and lived three years. He was sick and discouraged, and continued his way to Elgin, Kansas. Unrelenting misfortune met him at every turn. His children, as he believed, were predisposed to tuberculosis. On the other side of the Plains was Colorado with its mountain air and its pure water. Germaine yoked his oxen and once more started for the promised land.

Catherine Germaine, the oldest of the four captured sisters, has related the incidents of that journey and its final catastrophe in these words:

"We left Elgin August 10, 1874. We journeyed along till we came to the Smoky Hill River. Here we were told by the people living along the line that we had better keep along the river, so we could get water. They said we could not get water if we went along the railroad. And if we took the old trail by the river we would not see a house for over a hundred miles. We took the river road and everything seemed perfectly quiet. We met several persons on our several days' journey up the river.

"Father said we would start early and make Fort Wallace the last day. I knew that he felt uneasy all that lonely way, but we had no indications of danger, and now we were so near to the settlement he seemed more at ease.

"It was September 11. We were just starting as the sun began to peep over the hills. Father took his gun and started on ahead of the wagon. My brother and I had gone to drive the cows along. We were driving two cows and two yearlings. We had just turned them toward the moving wagon when we heard yells.

"On looking we saw Indians dashing down upon the wagon and father. We were about a hundred yards off and we started to run in an northeastern direction. We got something like a half mile but we were followed by the Indians. Brother was killed and I was taken back to the wagon, only to see that father, mother and my oldest sister had been killed. Then they killed my sister younger than me. They thought they were taking the four youngest because I was smaller than my sister they killed last. This was all done in a very short time.

"Leaving the wreck behind, they then started south, and took the cattle along some distance; then they killed them, ate what they wanted and left the carcasses lay. That afternoon a thunderstorm came up and the rain poured down, but we had no shelter. When they stopped for the night they tried to fix blankets up for shelter, but made a poor attempt at it. There were nineteen Indians, seventeen men and two squaws. The little squaw (we called her) seemed very sorry for us and would try to prepare something for us to eat, but the big one was of a different nature and not much inclined to do anything for our benefit. If anything was done to make our distress greater, she seemed to enjoy it hugely.

"These Indians had left their main tribe on the plains of Texas and come on a raiding tour. There was a raiding party of about a hundred in the country at that time. We did not see the big party."

"When an Indian war party moves rapidly over long distances in dangerous country, they become fagged just as do white men. When this band reached the Arkansas, a halt was made to forage for meat. Cattle were killed wherever they could be found, and the carcasses abandoned to wolves after the Indians had eaten their fill. The party seemed fearful that soldiers were following them.

"We traveled at a lively gait and I know they were expecting to be followed." They scarcely spoke above a whisper. We travelled speedily till toward morning, then stopped till daylight. We were pretty hungry some days, for we did not have our meals very regular; once a day and sometimes not that often. Julia and Addie, the little ones, were kept together. Sophia and I were not allowed to be together, though now and then we got together for a while. When we came to the Canadian River the Indians seemed very uneasy, and hid in the hills, hollows and brush for three days. The troops had been that way only a short time before we got there. The wagon trails were fresh yet. They left the Canadian on the third night and traveled nearly all night. Then for several days we traveled across the highland between the Canadian and Red rivers.

"When we came to the hills of the Red river they took to traveling at night again. We had been travelling on this night about two hours, and I should think it was somewhere about 11 o'clock, when all of a sudden they became confused and held a whispered consultation. Whatever their fright was, they went around it, and traveled at a very lively rate for a while. When they stopped to rest a little I was given permission to get off my horse. I was so tired I threw myself on the ground. When I lay there I thought I heard the distant barking of a dog and it made me feel glad to think that there might soon be a chance for the deliverance of us four helpless girls. We resumed our travelling till nearly day and stopped in a canyon. When I awoke the sun was shining around. They went up the canyon some distance, then came out on the prairie where thousands of buffalo were feeding. The buffalo did not seem to be very much afraid of any one. We were probably a mile from where we came out of the canyon. The Indians became greatly alarmed, saddled fresh horses and started in the direction we came, only a little more northwest.

"My little sisters were sitting on the ground. Two Indian men were there. These two Indians often carried them on their horses, and I thought that was what they would do now; but I wanted to see, so I held my horse back. They saw me lagging behind, so they came up and drove me on, but blamed the horse because he was lame and they thought he stayed of his own accord. After a while I saw those two Indians who were last with Julia and Addie, and also that my little sisters were not with them. I felt that we would all be better off if we were out of our misery, but I did not like to think of their little bodies being left out there for the buffalo to tramp over and the wolves to eat. As soon as I got a chance I told Sophia that they had killed Julia and Addie, and all she said was, 'They are better off than we are.' But God had a hand in that work, and I believe you will agree with me when I say he wrought a miracle and those little girls were taken care of. I never saw the little ones any more till June, 1875, when I met them at Fort Leavenworth."

After abandoning these two little girls, each of whom was less than ten years old, the Indians began pressing forward more rapidly than ever, to reach the vast solitudes of the Panhandle plains country, where the main body of Cheyennes had gone, and which the raiders reached after a three days' flight. The Cheyennes now divided into small parties, each going in different direction, to confuse the trails, and make pursuit by the soldiers difficult. Sophia and Catherine became separated, each going with a different band. Sophia was first in discovering that her two little sisters were alive—they had been found by other Indians. Julia said that she and Adelaide cried when they saw the Indians ride away, because they were afraid to be alone in such a strange wild place, and did not know where to find water or anything to eat. They stood in dread of the buffalo, hundreds of which were near at hand. As the Indians rode away, they motioned to the little girls to follow them. This they tried to do, but finally lost the trail. They were abandoned September 25. Sophia scarcely had time to embrace the little ones before she was carried away by the band that held her captive.

Julia and Addie were with Chief Gray Beard's band of Cheyennes. General Miles was pressing the Indians upon all sides. His command was superior to the combined forces of all the hostiles in the Southwest and the latter could have been annihilated in a single engagement had it been possible to attack them in a position where their only alternative would have been to fight their way out. But the Indians were too shrewd to be caught in a trap, and were running and dodging in every direction, their trails crossing and re-crossing and doubling back and turning aside until they were a confused jumble. The Indians knew the country as accurately as a coyote knows the course to its den. The only fact plain to the scouts was that the hostiles were trying to escape to the Staked Plains. In this uninhabited and practically waterless region a large body of troops would have been badly handicapped in its pursuit of small bands of the enemy, as the latter could move more rapidly and with greater comfort, and in time exhaust the endurance of troops traveling in more or less compact formation.

General Miles embraced every opportunity to employ the tactics of the Indians, and it was the result of this kind of strategy that brought Lieutenant Baldwin and his scouts within striking distance of Gray Beard's band on McClellan Creek.

The Indians were so hard pressed that they were forced to abandon Julia and Adelaide and much camp equipment. I remember vividly the appearance of the deserted camp. We had ridden almost past it when somebody noticed that a pile of buffalo hides seemed to be moving up and down. Pulling the hides aside, we were astonished at finding two little white girls, who proved to be Julia and Adelaide. They were pitiable objects. Hunger and privation had reduced them to mere skeletons, and their little hands and fingers were so thin that they resembled bird's claws. The children were trembling with fright, but upon seeing that we were white men their terror changed to a frenzy of joy, and their sobs and tears made hardened frontiersmen turn away to hide their own emotion. The children said that they had not been mistreated by the men. The squaws, however, had forced them to work beyond their strength. The little girls were sent to Fort Leavenworth. Their rescue took place November 8, 1874.

Catherine and Sophia Germaine were now far out on the Staked Plains. We had fought the Indians—principally Cheyennes, with a few Kiowas—at Tule Canyon, a branch of Red River, but without capturing them. General Miles, fearful that the two captives might be wantonly killed by the Indians, when the latter found themselves in increasing danger of attack or capture, employed a Mexican mixed-blood at Fort Sill to go to the hostile camp in the Staked Plains with a secret message to the Germaine girls telling them Julia and Adelaide were safe and in the hands of friends and not to become discouraged. This message fell into the hands of Catherine. It was written on the back of a photograph of Julia and Adelaide that had been made by W. P. Bliss, shortly after they were found by Lieutenant Baldwin's command.

The Cheyennes that had fled to the Staked Plains were under the redoubtable Chief Stone Calf. General Miles sent a formal demand for surrender to Stone Calf, with the specific provision that Catherine and Sophia Germaine should be brought back alive. Stone Calf and his followers surrendered March 1, 1875, about seventy-five miles west of the Darlington Indian Agency.

"Just before the sun set," wrote Catherine Germaine, "we came to the soldiers' camp. They stood at the side of the trail cheering. We stopped, but I could hardly say anything and when I think of it now a lump rises in my throat. Oh, I was so glad. I thought I had never seen such white people. They looked as white as snow, but of course they were no whiter than the average people, but my being accustomed to the red people was why they seemed so white and pretty. I just lacked a few days of being eighteen years old when we were recaptured, and Sophia was past twelve. We were at the Cheyenne Agency (Darlington) three months."

A Panhandle Dugout

The warriors who surrendered with Stone Calf were stood in a row by General Miles, and the Germaine girls asked to point out those who had engaged in the murder of the other members of the Germaine family, or who had mistreated the captives. They pointed out seventy-five Indians, all of whom afterwards were sent to Florida as prisoners of war.

General Miles induced the United States government to appropriate the sum of $10,000 for the benefit of the four girls. He was their guardian for two or three years. They were educated at the expense of the military branch of the Government. All the girls married, and some of them are still living.

The Miles Campaign demonstrated that if there should be further Indian outbreaks it would be well to have a garrison within easy striking distance of the route that led to the Staked Plains. Fort Elliott was established as a permanent garrison in the spring of 1875. I was with the party that selected the site. I was attached as scout at Fort Elliott, and remained in service at that place until 1883. I was the last scout to be relieved of duty at that post, and when I went away the buffalo was becoming a rare animal on the Plains and the Indian was down and out.

Much has been said about the killing of horses, in 1874, by the troops of Colonel McKenzie's command. The facts are Colonel McKenzie had whipped the Indians out of the canyons and had driven them to the Staked Plains, south of what is known as Tulia (the old Spanish word was "tule" and meant cat-tail, reed, or flag). The Indians were supposed to have twelve thousand horses of all sorts, most of which had been stolen from the whites. Colonel McKenzie's men would capture large numbers of horses from them in the daytime and the Comanches and Kiowas would steal them back at night, for he was not able to hold them. Being determined to get them afoot (to get an Indian afoot means to get him whipped), he captured what he could of the horses and ordered them shot. Colonel McKenzie and the troops who were with him generally estimated the number of horses thus shot at about thirteen hundred.

Cattlemen began going into the Panhandle as the Indians went out. I remember how greatly I was surprised when I arrived at the Goodnight ranch one day in 1877, and found two white ladies—Mrs. Goodnight, who had joined her husband the previous year, and Mrs. Willingham, whose husband was afterwards superintendent of the Turkey Track Ranch. Both were refined, educated women. I often think how helpful such women as Mrs. Goodnight and Mrs. Willingham have been to Panhandle communities. It required some grit for men to live there in those days, and for women the trials and burdens must have been disheartening.

The Staked Plains, by reason of the scarcity of water in summer, opposed great danger to troops in moving through that part of the country. I was with Captain Nicholas Nolan, in command of Troop A, Tenth United States Cavalry, in that memorable experience in August, 1877, in which the detachment barely escaped death from thirst. Captain Nolan was in pursuit of the Quahada band of Comanches, who had slipped away from their reservation at Fort Sill, Indian Territory. Far out on the Staked Plains we joined forces with a party of buffalo-hunters who had organized to fight the Indians. Captain Nolan told the buffalo-hunters that if they would help him find the Indians he would agree to do all the fighting, and assured them that he would do the work to their satisfaction.

Reports were brought in that the Indians were only a short distance away, and that it might be possible to overtake them by moving quickly. In the excitement, many of the soldiers as well as the buffalo-hunters forgot to fill their canteens with water. The Indians eluded us, the men were soon out of water, and a difference of opinion arose as to where the nearest water could be found. Some were in favor of trying for the Double Lakes and some for the Laguna Plata. I had been over this country from the north, not from the direction we were traveling. The men and horses were in a deplorable condition.

Captain Nolan told Lieutenant Cooper to take the course with his compass, which was set east by south ten degrees. The buffalo-hunters feared the distance was too great, and started in another direction, for Laguna Plata. Captain Nolan thought the Double Lakes were further west than I did. We argued over the route until about 3 o'clock in the afternoon, when he told me to go the way I thought was right. I at once turned more to the northeast. About 5 o'clock I waved my hat to attract the attention of the command, and an orderly came forward. I sent word to Captain Nolan that I thought I saw the Double Lakes. Happily, I was not mistaken. We had to dig for water, and 11 o'clock had passed before the horses were able to quench their thirst.

When the negro troopers came up and saw water they plainly showed their relief and pleasure. Several of them said with a broad grin, "Mr. Dixon, we would follow you anywhere. You sure am the best guide we ever saw."

The Indians we were following eluded us on the Staked Plains and we were unable to get trace of them. The summer was unusually dry and hot. The Indians had every advantage; they knew the country and we did not.

An officer's wife at Fort Elliott, whose husband was among the last men to come in, had her hair turn gray in one night when a couple of soldiers returned to the fort and reported the men all dead. (The soldiers who told this story were court-martialed and sent to the penitentiary for two years.)

The sufferings of both men and horses were terrible, and all the way to the Double Lakes our trail was strewn with cast-off clothing and equipment. The buffalo-hunters were in no less desperate straits, many of them, like the soldiers, dropping down to die along the way. Horses were killed that their blood might be drunk to assuage the fever of burning throats and tongues. The buffalo-hunters finally reached water at the Casa Amarilla. Both outfits carried water back to fallen comrades and revived them.

Dr. J. L. Powell, an assistant surgeon stationed at Camp Supply, in 1878, was a great fellow to hunt and a splendid shot. He was a native of Virginia and talked with a rich southern accent. In speaking to his horse, he would say: "whoa, sar!

I often went hunting with Doctor Powell. He could beat me shooting at a target but he had never been able to shoot a deer. Like many other men I have known, when he saw a deer, he became very much excited and took the buck ague. At this time deer were plentiful. One day during the fall of 1878, the Doctor and I went out on a small creek near Camp Supply to hunt. On reaching a small draw which led off from the creek, Doctor Powell said: "Dixon, you go on up the creek and I will follow this draw." I saw that he wanted to be alone and did as he instructed. Following the creek a short distance, I came in sight of seven deer quietly grazing in the valley. I shot and wounded, what later proved to be the leader, a big fine buck. I had broken his front leg. At the report of my rifle they ran, but on seeing their leader stop the rest did likewise, running ahead for a distance. Leaving the one first shot until the last, I killed all seven deer.

Going over on the draw, I found Doctor Powell looking somewhat disappointed. "Well, Doctor, what luck?" "I haven't seen a deer" he replied. "What luck did you have?" "I saw seven and killed them all." The Doctor refused to believe this, thinking it was a joke until we returned to camp and I asked the cook to hook up a team and go out with me to bring in seven deer that I had just killed.

Doctor Powell went out with us. Afterward he was more fortunate and I had the satisfaction of seeing him bring down many a fine buck.

CHAPTER XIII

RETURNING to civilian life in 1883, I struck north from Fort Elliott and went over on the Canadian River, in what is now Hutchinson County, Texas, and hired to a big cow outfit that became widely known as the Turkey Track Ranch, owned by a Scotch syndicate, and then managed by C. B. Willingham. That same year I filed on three sections of land on Bent Creek, taking in the site of the original Adobe Walls ruins. I built my house right at the west edge of the old stockade building, which by that time stock had rubbed to the ground. In the front yard, however, when the south wind swept the dirt clear of sand, could still be seen the foundations of the old ruins. Whoever built those walls certainly built them well.

When I homesteaded my two sections of school land and built my house at Adobe Walls, I expected to live there the balance of my days, contented and happy. Everything was to my liking— pure air, good water, fruitful soil, game, and room enough for a man to turn round without stepping on some fellow's toes. It was the land of my boyhood dreams, and I was satisfied.

I improved my ranch in many ways. I diverted the course of Bent Creek until its clear, swift waters flowed almost at my doorstep, and was able to undertake extensive irrigation. I planted an orchard of 200 carefully selected trees, consisting of apples, peaches, pears, plums, apricots and cherries, together with a small vineyard. I am confident that this was the first orchard ever planted in Hutchinson County, perhaps in the northern Panhandle. It was well irrigated, and the orchard thrived astonishingly. In the yard I set out a number of cottonwoods, which grew rapidly and became big, strong trees, affording generous shade in hot summer. I am sure that my thirty acres of alfalfa was the first ever seen in that section. For many years it produced an unfailing and profitable crop.

In those days our nearest postoffice was Zulu, on Palo Duro Creek in Hansford County, twenty-five or thirty miles to the northwest. One day L. D. Miller, then district attorney, later a lawyer at Allenreed, Texas, was at the Turkey Track Ranch. He heard about the way we had to go for mail, and said that he would have a postoffice established at the ranch and make me postmaster. I received my commission and was postmaster at Adobe Walls for nearly twenty years, first at the ranch and later at my home. When I moved down to my own place I opened a little store, carrying in stock such simple things as would supply cowboy trade. It may cause a smile when I say that my two most important articles of merchandise were candy and chewing gum. No schoolgirl could be as foolish as a cowboy about candy and chewing gum.

BILLY DIXON IN LATER YEARS

The boys seemed to crave such things, and bought more candy and chewing gum than they did tobacco.

The illustration of the bluff on the east side of Adobe Walls Creek gives an excellent view of the landscape. In coming to attack Adobe Walls in the early morning, the Indians rode up the valley from the right, and were first discovered near the grove of trees.

Mine was a happy life in my cabin at Adobe Walls, without fret or worry, and with abundance of everything for my simple needs. During a greater part of the year wild ducks and geese frequented the Canadian and its tributaries, literally by thousands, and deer and turkey were commonly found along the creeks.

The meat of the buffalo, in my opinion, had a much better taste than beef, and was more easily digested. I was always a big meat eater, and often long for a good fat buffalo steak broiled over a camp-fire in the way "Frenchie," my old cook, used to broil it. When we were camped on a creek where wild turkeys were plentiful, we would kill fifteen or twenty and stew a potful of gizzards, hearts and livers. This was best of all, a dish fit for a king, and a man who never ate it can have no idea how good it was.

I lived here as a bachelor until I married in 1894, after which I continued at Adobe Walls until about 1902, when I sold my ranch and moved to Plemons, Texas. There I lived two years, and found living in town worse than it could have been in jail. I decided to go still further west, and in 1906 home-steaded a claim in what was then known as Beaver County, Oklahoma, once called "No Man's Land." My place was in sight of Buffalo Springs, and on the north line of the Panhandle. My house set just far enough on the Oklahoma side to hold the land.

A change in local conditions began in 1887. In that year a good many "nesters," small stockmen, began coming in and taking up the land. They were bitterly opposed by the big cow outfits, none of which wanted to see the country fenced, and felt that the settlers were intruding into a country where they did not belong and where they certainly were not wanted. I rather think that the cow out-fits felt that they had won the country from the In-dians and were entitled to it by right of conquest and occupancy. But the "nesters" forced the cow outfits to leave, just as the buffalo-hunters and the soldiers had made the Indians depart. Today the despised "nester" is the bone and sinew of the Pan-handle country, and whatever social and material advancement the country has made should be credited mostly to those who built homes and school houses and churches, and tamed the wild land to the crops of civilization. I do not wish to say anything against the cowmen. They were big hearted, generous fellows, who followed their own way as they saw it. Between the two classes there was much conflict; time, however, solves its problems, and it has solved them in the Panhandle.

In 1874 Thomas O'Loughlin and his wife, Ellen,

left Pierceville, Kansas, where they had owned a small grocery store, determined to seek their fortune to the southwest. They decided to come to the Panhandle, and learning that Fort Elliott, where the present town of Mobeetie now stands, was established, they loaded two wagons with merchandise and all their personal possessions and began the long trip over an Indian-infested land.

Mrs. O'Loughlin drove one of the wagons and her husband the other. When they reached the Canadian River near Cantonment Creek, a party of soldiers who were camped near helped them across. After reaching Fort Elliott they built a picket house and Mrs. O'Loughlin kept boarders in connection with her husband's grocery store.

J. W. Kelley moved his family into the Panhandle in 1887, settling on Wolf Creek in Lipscomb County, where he owns a ranch of eighteen (18) sections of land today. Doctors were scarce in the early days, and Mrs. Kelley used to make long rides on horseback and in buggies to wait on the sick.

Besides the Kelleys, other small stockmen who moved their families to the Panhandle in 1887 were Lards, Ledricks and Walstads, all coming down from Kansas. The Lard and Ledrick families located on Chicken Creek. The Walstad family lived first on Wolf Creek, moving later to the "flats" in Ochiltree County. The Walstads were sturdy Norwegians and not afraid to work. To improve their place on the "flats," they cut cedar pickets in Government Canyon, ten miles away, and "snaked" them up the steep bluffs with a horse; the place was too rough for a team to descend. Nevertheless, they constructed a good-sized, comfortable dwelling out of these pickets, and covered it with dirt. Water was scarce on the "flats," the Walstads hauling it ten or fifteen miles the first year. Mr. Walstad undertook to dig a well by hand, something that no man before nor since has ever tried in that country. He was not financially able to bore a well, and did not know that it was anywhere from 300 to 400 feet to water. He got down about 200 feet and threw up the sponge—the sponge was dry.

The girls in the Walstad family were all splendid riders, and could rope a cow or a horse as easily as a man. They rode long distances after stock in all kinds of weather.

The Lards and Ledricks prospered on Chicken Creek. Henry Ledrick had been a post-trader in Kansas, and had lost all his property as the result of Indian raids. The Government afterward compensated him for his losses. By intermarriage these families have established themselves in many of the Panhandle counties.

For years I was justice of the peace in Hutchinson County. The hardest job I ever tackled was to perform a marriage ceremony, though I married many couples. Ministers were as scarce as buffalo, and when a couple decided to get married they went to the nearest justice of the peace or county judge. My usual embarrassment in marrying a couple was once increased beyond measure. I had grown to be very fond of a young lady who lived with Mrs. Willingham on the Turkey Track Ranch, but had never been able to muster courage to tell her how much I thought of her and to ask her to marry me. Well, a pesky cowboy did what I had not been able to do, and the two came to have me tie the conjugal knot. I thought that it was hard enough to lose the girl, but to be asked to marry her to another fellow was certainly tough.

Some of the large outfits controlled entire counties for range purposes—and the Panhandle counties were big counties. The Hansford Land & Cattle Company (the Turkey Track Ranch) ran 50,000 head of cattle at one time, and ranged over three counties—Hansford, Hutchinson and Roberts.

The Turkey Track Ranch tried to escape the inevitable by buying out "nesters" who came into the country in the late 80's, and in this way held all the land, save mine at Adobe Walls. The Texas legislature opened up the land to purchase and settlement, and in the 90's the settlers began coming and could not be stopped. They settled first along the creeks and then spread to the uplands. I was State land commissioner for Hutchinson County and did a thriving business.

The people petitioned the Legislature that Hutchinson County be detached from Roberts County, and given a separate organization. Their petition was granted. An election was called for the election of county officers. Much ill feeling had grown up between the settlers and the cow outfits, especially the Turkey Track people, who had opposed the making of a new county. The election was bitterly contested, the Turkey Track outfit taking an active part, to control the results. I was elected sheriff, not because I sought the office, but because I had lived in the country so long that I was widely known. I was ignorant of politics and the ways of politicians. I became disgusted and resigned my office, rather than be forced into strife that was not to my liking, and went back to the quietude of Adobe Walls. The county judge, Harry Ingerton, also resigned. When a man gets mixed up in politics he is soon traveling a rocky road.

However, I do not hold enmity against anybody. Many changes have taken place in Hutchinson County since that time, and today it is settled with law-abiding, prosperous stockmen and farmers. The Turkey Track sold out to a Kansas company, who also bought my place at Adobe Walls.

I married Miss Olive King in 1894. She had come from Virginia to visit her brothers, Albert and Archie King, and the winter before we were married she had taught school on the south side of the Canadian, between Reynolds and Tallahone creeks. This school house was built of round cottonwood logs covered with dirt, and was about twelve feet square.

There were no desks or modern fixtures. A barrel of drinking water was hauled once a week. There were large cracks between the logs and when the weather got cold the teacher and pupils chinked and daubed the walls to keep out the cold. These were little things, however, to a young woman in love with the West and her surroundings, and later on my wife often remarked that this was one of the happiest years of her life.

I had always been rather bashful in the presence of women, rarely having had opportunity to meet them in a social way. Merely the sight of a good-looking woman coming in my direction made me feel like leaving the trail. How I ever managed to ask my wife to marry me has always been a mystery, made even more remarkable by the fact that she consented. I have always insisted that she did the proposing, but could say no more when she reminded me of the time we were riding together and watered our horses at Garden Creek Springs, one September afternoon, and of the promise I made her at that time.

We were married October 18, 1894, on Reynolds Creek at the home of a Portugese family named Lewis, where my wife had boarded during the winter. The Lewises were running about 200 head of cattle and had a comfortable home. Mrs. Lewis was a cultivated woman. She spoke English brokenly, and to make herself more familiar with the language had induced my wife to live with her. Mrs. Lewis had been a good friend of mine for several years, and I suspect that it was largely through her influence that I got the girl I so greatly admired.

We have been living together nearly nineteen years. She has borne me a family of which I feel that I am justly proud, and has stood by me in all my ups and downs. It is largely through her efforts that these reminiscences have been written. I never took the interest that I should take in setting down these matters, and I realize that the work should have been done years ago.

We were married by a Methodist minister, the Rev. C. V. Bailey, who drove seventy-five miles from Mobeetie to perform the ceremony. After our marriage, my wife for a period of three years was the only woman who actually lived in Hutchinson County. She may have grown a bit lonesome, but if she did she never said anything about it. I had the advantage of being able to say, without making any other man angry, that I had the best looking woman in the County. It was not every woman who had lived in a thickly settled community all her life that would have been willing to settle down at Adobe Walls.

When Patten, Price & Hyde, the Kansas cattlemen, bought the Turkey Track range and stock, I sold my place at Adobe Walls to them. My older children by this time were in need of schooling. The settlers were so few that there was no neighborhood school; so we moved to Plemons and lived there for two years before locating in Cimarron

AN ADOBE CORRAL BUILT BY BILLY DIXON

County, then Beaver County, which is settled by the best type of rugged American citizenship. They are temperate, law-abiding, industrious people. Most of them were poor at the beginning, and many have had a hard time getting started. All have the true western spirit. If a settler is in trouble, caused by sickness, death or other unavoidable misfortune, his neighbors are always ready to help him, even putting in his crops for him.

I am often questioned about my experiences on the frontier, as if the life had been filled with unbearable hardships, to be shunned and forgotten. Gladly would I live it all over again, such is my cast of mind and my hunger for the freedom of the big wide places. I would run the risks and endure all the hardships that were naturally ours just for the contentment and freedom to be found in such an outdoor life. I should be unspeakably happy once more to feast on buffalo meat and other wild game cooked on a camp-fire, to eat sour dough biscuit and drink black coffee from a quart tin cup.

But those days are gone forever, and we must content ourselves with the present and make the best of our opportunities. Coming generations will never know the trials and hardships we endured. We helped build a great empire in the West.

Let it be governed justly and made to serve the needs of humanity.

THE END.

INDEX